SHARED PRE
PRESEN

M000192448

THE
BODHISATTVA
AND THE
SPACE AGE

THE GREAT IDEA IN OUR TIME

ROGER WEIR

SHARED PRESENCE
FOUNDATION

Shared Presence Foundation Presentation Series
The Bodhisattva and the Space Age: The Great Idea in Our Time
(March 2021)

Access complementary digital media (audio, video, and documents) related to this book by scanning the code below.

https://sharedpresencefoundation.org/bsa

More digital media related to the work of Roger Weir is available at: https://sharedpresencefoundation.org

© 2021 Shared Presence Foundation
1st ed.
Library of Congress Cataloging-in-Publication Data
A catalogue record for this book is available from the Library of Congress
ISBN: 978-1-7358769-5-5 (hardcover)
ISBN: 978-1-7358769-3-1 (paperback)
ISBN: 978-1-7358769-4-8 (e-book)
Library of Congress Control Number: 2021902702

In appreciation of
Roger Allen Weir
1940-2018

ACKNOWLEDGEMENTS

The editors would like to express a deep gratitude to all those individuals who have committed their time to assist in editing, revising, and publishing this text. Without your contributions we could not have fully realized this publication.

"The great failure of the 20th Century was the failure to disseminate the great developments in science and art to the masses. Only through an education tuning man to East and West — to the crème de la crème of Art, History, and Science throughout civilization — can we seek to recalibrate this."

Roger Weir

CONTENTS

Figure 1. Photo of the Kuan Yin statue on Mount Putuo, Zhousan, China. Mount Putuo is one of four sacred mountains in Chinese Buddhism. (Photograph by Ferdinand Feng, Unsplash).

PREFACE

The Bodhisattva and the Space Age: The Great Idea In Our Time is an edited transcript of a presentation given by Roger Weir at the Philosophical Research Society in Los Angeles, California on September 12, 1982.

To attend one of Roger Weir's presentations was to enter into a new form of learning exploration. To attend them regularly was life-changing. In 2011, The Shared Presence Foundation was created to preserve and share Weir's works, and now, even since his passing in 2018, his legacy lives on.

The text includes a number of important terms which at their first occurrence appear in **bold.** The definitions for these terms can be found in the Key Terms section located at the back of the book.

The Shared Presence Foundation intends to provide the teachings and presentations of Weir in multimedia formats, including audio and video when possible, as well as through this Presentations Series of books and ebooks. Digital media related to the work of Roger Weir is available at: https://sharedpresencefoundation.org

INTRODUCTION
HOW TO USE THIS BOOK

Adapted from its original format, published here for the first time, Roger Weir's *The Bodhisattva and the Space Age: The Great Idea in Our Time*, which blends the ancient Buddhist writings with a modern cosmic understanding, guiding the learner on a journey through time and space.

The Bodhisattva and the Space Age is an exploration of the relationship between cultural and spiritual traditions, as well as an introduction to a new way of considering the nuances of their similarities and distinctions. It tells of the story of the creation of *The Awakening of Faith in Mahayana*, and the indelible alteration it left on human consciousness. Weir weaves together the historical context of pivotal turning points in civilization, and acknowledges an "iconographical correlation" between the Christian Mother Mary, the Buddhist Goddess Kuan Yin, and the Egyptian Goddess Isis, inspiring and exciting the creative imagination.

The message does not end there. Weir thoughtfully leads the learner through an introduction to the uniquely enlightened layman, Yuima (also known as Vimalakirti) through the *Vimalakirtinirdesa Sutra*, touching then upon the significance of the *Accumulation of*

Precious Qualities, and landing in the modern space age, weaving these ancient stories and ideas into the cosmic understanding of infinite galaxies beyond our own.

In *The Bodhisattva and the Space Age*, you'll explore:

- ***The Awakening of Faith in the Mahayana (Shraddhotpada Mahayana Sutra)*** – Learn the eight reasons for the creation of the revolutionary text and the shift in Buddhist consciousness from a personal liberation to a universal liberation through the introduction of the goddess Kuan Yin, the bodhisattva of compassion.
- ***The Teaching of Vimalakirti (Vimalakirtinirdesa Sutra)*** – Discover one of the most famous of the Mahayana Sutras, which tells the story of Yuima (also known as Vimalakirti), a layman whose wisdom surprised and amazed even some of the most famous Buddhas and bodhisattvas in history.
- ***The Accumulation of Precious Qualities (Prajna Paramita Ratna Guna Samcaya Gatha)*** – The paradise of the Amitabha Buddha is not one of just singing and mindlessness, but one of study and great erudition because the bodhisattva ideal includes omniscience – one must know it all – every bit of it, in all of its ramifications, for all beings to learn.
- **The Space Age** – The modern scientific worldview reveals that there are infinite galaxies in all directions around ours, and from a Buddhist perspective, they are peopled with infinite beings in need of liberation from the cycle of samsara.

From a practical perspective, this book can be used as a study complement to the audio presentation available at the Shared Presence Foundation website. With the illustrations and maps, the reader can deepen their connection to the ideas and messages discussed. With the transcribed word, the student can contemplate on their meaning, and stay with the content longer than in a pre-recorded audio. The audio recording of *The Bodhisattva and the Space Age: The Great Idea In Our Time* by Roger Weir is available at no cost on the Shared Presence Foundation website.

Access complementary digital media (audio, video, and documents) related to this book by scanning the code below.

https://sharedpresencefoundation.org/bsa

Figure 2. A scroll painting by an unknown artist depicting the goddess of compassion, Kuan Yin, seated on lotus flowers amongst the clouds. (Wikimedia Commons).

PART I
AWAKENING OF FAITH IN THE MAHAYANA

The goddess **Kuan Yin** is perhaps the most famous **bodhisattva** in East Asia. She is the graceful lady of the Orient. She's related in iconographical background to Isis in the ancient world, or the Virgin Mary in our modern Western world.

Kuan Yin, in the scroll,[1] has in one hand a leafy green flower stock which in many other versions has blossomed out into a chrysanthemum — or more often a lotus. In the hand, which she has extended, she has a flower vase that is long and elegant, with sort of a milky opalescence. From this, she is pouring a milky fluid, which falls in the continuous waterfall, down to a bubble at her feet. Usually, the bubble is just suspended in space. And her feet have sandals, which have cloud motifs on the base of them. We are given to understand that she stands beyond any gravitational exercise, beyond any electromagnetic context, which we might envision.

---

[1] The description of the scroll provided by Weir is of a scroll featuring Kuan Yin from the personal collection of Manly P. Hall — which was not able to be included here at the time of publication.

Within the bubble is a child, and the child has its knees raised in a fetal position. Its hands are brought together in an adoration position. Sort of the **gassho.** And the only difference from a fetal position is that the head is raised and craned backwards to look off at Kuan Yin. The mouth is open in an adoration of sound, or singing, or cooing, or in some metaphysical mantric posture.

This image was used without the Kuan Yin, and with a difference within the posture of the baby, as the last frame in a science fiction movie about 15 years ago, called *2001* [*2001: A Space Odyssey* (1968)]. It's at the end of that movie. At the end of the movie, the child within the bubble floats above the planet Earth, and in the hazy shine of the blue air, fading into the dark depths of space, we see the face and posture of man born anew. This was the image that Stanley Kubrick, the maker of the film, and Arthur C. Clarke, the author of the screenplay, chose to exemplify — the crucial final transformation of man in our time.

I think both Mr. Hall and I prefer the old Kuan Yin version, where the child is actually not just a blank-eyed baby but is one full of adoration, knowing its origins and understanding that its nurturing and fruition comes from a universal space mother, who appears to our finite minds as a life-sustaining goddess, full of grace and beauty. And exemplifying compassion in its universal sense.

Figure 3. A triptych of (left to right) the Egyptian goddess Isis, the Buddhist bodhisattva Kuan Yin, and the Christian Blessed Virgin Mary. Illustration of Isis from, *The Sacred Books and Early Literature of the East,* vol. 2 – Egypt (New York: Parke, Austin, and Lipscomb, 1917), between p. 96 and 97; Picture of Kuan Yin statue by Ferdinand Feng, Unsplash; Painting of the Blessed Virgin Mary by Leopold Kupolwieser from St. Peter's Church, Vienna, Austria as photographed by Adam Jan Figel (Shutterstock) in June 2020.

Where does all this come from? How is it that this wonderful insight and doctrine comes to have been expressed through every country in Asia is, in fact, the golden thread, the tie line, which unites all of the Asian traditions together, and seems to find some sympathetic reverberation in our time, separated so far in geographical distance. So far in cultural development. So distant in supposed purposes of life.

For this story, we have to take ourselves and our imagination back to a time, about the time of the apostles in the West, 1st century CE, and the scene is Northern India. There was, at that time, a very great king named **Kanishka.** And Kanishka was the founder of what is known in history as the **Kushan** empire. The Kushan empire was an enormous construct — one of the largest empires of its time — rivaling the Roman empire on one side and the Chinese Han empire on the other. Those three empires together, incidentally, girded the known world at that time. And only the Americas were excluded from the hegemony of those three civilizations.

Kanishka had spread the Kushan empire from its rude beginnings as a Chinese tribe in outer Mongolia. In Chinese, it's called the **Yuezhi** tribe. They had migrated through various internal pressures and desires into an area known as Kashmir. They're in the Southern part of Kashmir — the Northern part of Pakistan today — at a city, which we call today Peshawar, they called Purusapura at that time, they founded the capital of the Kushan empire. It stretched from South central India — Hyderabad and Mysore — all the way through India, through Pakistan, through Afghanistan, up into the Karakum Desert. So-called Karakum because of the black sands there.[2] It's today, Chinese Turkestan or several of the Uzbek provinces of central Soviet Asia,[3] and a stretch from the Bamiyan

---

[2] In Turkic languages (i.e., Turkish, Azerbaijani, Turkmen) 'karakum' means 'black sand'.

[3] This includes the following nations: Kazakhstan, Kyrgyzstan, Tajikistan, Turkmenistan, and Uzbekistan.

Valley,[4] leading from Afghanistan into Persia, all the way to the sacred city of **Patna**[5] on the Ganges [River], far over to East India.

All of this empire was controlled by one great king, who in 78 CE gathered together his mighty armies: huge populations of elephants that were decorated with enormous pampas grass plumes; huge carriages that were drawn by these elephants; large series of mounted horsemen; an army of several hundred thousand persons. With great entourage, dignity, and power, Kanishka surrounded the sacred city of Patna, ringed it completely around several times and demanded from the residents of Patna their most sacred treasure. To forestall any death upon his part or any violence on the account of his being, the most sacred treasure of Patna voluntarily walked out of the city and joined Kanishka's troop. This was the Buddhist monk named **Ashvaghosha.**[6]

Ashvaghosha, who, with his little begging bowl and his saffron robe and bare head, walked out of Patna. The huge entourage of several hundred thousand turned and wheeled on its pinions, and in huge clouds of conch shells blowing sound, and dust, and pageantry, and regalia, Kanishka retreated back to his capital city of Peshawar with his treasure.

Why would a Buddhist monk, a single human being, be considered by so great a king of such a vast empire to be the greatest

---

[4] Bamiyan is the common English spelling. Other forms include, Bamyan or Bamian.

[5] Patna is the modern-day name for the ancient city of **Pataliputra** (see entry for Pataliputra in the Key Terms section).

[6] The spelling of Ashvaghosha's name varies, thus the editors have decided to use the most common non-diacritical, phonetic form: Ashvaghosha.

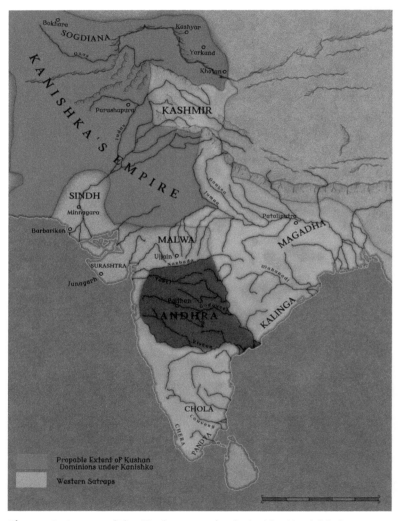

Figure 4. A map of the Kushan empire (ruled by Kanishka) depicting its extent circa 127–150 CE. Map art by Vojtěch Burian, 2020.

treasure? Ashvaghosha became the author of a single little pamphlet — translated, its title, the **Shraddhotpada Mahayana Sutra,** means *The Awakening of Faith in the Mahayana.*[7] It was the beginning, the first great expression of the idea that Buddhism had changed, had turned on its pinions, which had been the same for 500 or 600 years. It had finally redirected itself from a religion, which was concerned with passing on a sacred oral tradition of single self-salvation from one to another. It had transformed itself into a cosmic universal religion whose goal — expressed in the name **Mahayana,** 'The Greater Vehicle' — was that no one should rest, no one should selfishly seek for their own salvation until all other beings in the universe had likewise been saved. So, the transformation was from a personal salvation to one of universal salvation. The pinpoint upon which the whole pivot turned was the monk Ashvaghosha. In a single phrase, in the middle of his slender pamphlet — the *Shraddhotpada Mahayana Sutra* — was the glint of that pinpoint of the fulcrum of the turning. It was a phrase, which included the word, **tathata.** *Tathata,* in **Sanskrit,** translated into English, means 'suchness'. 'Suchness', the entire quality of religious experience and its expression in human life, and human aspiration from the individual to the cosmic turns about upon the understanding, and the appreciation — that well-worn consideration — of the meaning of *tathata,* suchness.

---

[7]   The true authorship of this sutra has been questioned by modern scholars, including Jan Nattier, Robert E. Buswell, and others. Currently, the general consensus among Buddhist scholars is that this sutra was originally a Chinese composition — not Sanskrit as previously believed — thus it is no longer attributed to Ashvaghosha. This scholarly consensus developed in the 1990s through research into the source material. Weir's presentation pre-dates this consensus, thus it does not reflect this scholarly consensus. For more information see the entry for *Shraddhotpada Mahayana Sutra (The Awakening of Faith in the Mahayana)* in the Key Terms section.

Ashvaghosha, in *The Awakening of Faith* at the very beginning, after he makes a homage to all those who have come before him — to the historical Buddha, to the continuing **sangha**, or brotherhood or fellowship, and to the individual **Dharma** that had been well-taught and preserved to his time — then explains eight reasons why he sought to write this document. He does not mention in the eight reasons that he was held captive, that he was a prisoner of Kanishka, because none of these were truthful reasons or motivations for Ashvaghosha. His truthful reasons were expressed in this document. He wrote, and this is a translation from Columbia University Press, the following:

> Someone may ask the reasons why I was led to write this treatise. I reply: there are eight reasons. The first and the main reason is to cause men to free themselves from all sufferings and to gain the final bliss; it is not that I desire worldly fame, material profit, or respect and honor.[8]

So, the first reason was so that human beings may cause themselves to be free from the world of sufferings. In Sanskrit, **samsara.**

> The second reason is that I wished to interpret the fundamental meaning of the teachings of the Tathagata so that men may understand them correctly and not be mistaken about them.[9]

---

[8]   Yoshito S. Hakeda, trans., *The Awakening of Faith* (New York: Columbia University Press, 1967), p. 25; Yoshito S. Hakeda, trans., *The Awakening of Faith*, BDK English Tripitaka 63-IV (Berkeley, California: Numata Center for Buddhist Translation and Research, 2005), p. 5, https://bdkamerica.org/product/the-awakening-of-faith/.
[9]   Ibid.

Here, instead of using the word Buddha, Ashvaghosha used, for the first time, another word — a word related to suchness, a word related to the word *tathata*. He called the Buddha the **tathagata**. This means, "he who has gone," or, "he who has *tathata* to the extent that it has saturated totally his being." Total suchness is one who has gone from this world of materiality and suffering. So, as his second reason, he wrote,

> I wish to interpret the fundamental meaning of the teachings of the Tathagata so that men may understand them correctly and not be mistaken about them.[10]

The third reason, very simple,

> To enable those whose capacity for goodness has attained maturity to keep firm hold upon an unretrogressive faith in the teachings of Mahayana.[11]

Because goodness has to mature; it doesn't just occur, it must be nourished, and it must grow. In other words, by his time, there was a sufficient population of persons, not just monks in a monastic community, but lay people everywhere in the world at large, in the material world, people for whom families and working were a normal daily procedure. Within the home, the capacity for goodness had matured to a sufficient extent that the greatest mind of his day turned his back on the monastic community. He saw the presence of the emperor of the world empire of the Kushan as an opportunity to teach and present the larger doctrine. This population of lay persons had grown to such an extent by the time of the

---

[10] Ibid.
[11] Ibid.

1st century CE in India, that Ashvaghosha felt this was the third reason for writing *The Awakening of Faith in the Mahayana.*

His fourth reason was,
> To encourage those whose capacity for goodness is still slight to cultivate the faithful mind.[12]

That is, for those who would like to have had the capacity for goodness, and in some far intuition or in some secret purpose intuit, or like to think that they would have that capacity but don't attribute it to themselves. At least they could be encouraged to cultivate what Ashvaghosha calls, 'the faithful mind'. There is a wonderful phrase at that time called **bodhicitta**, that is, 'the seed of enlightenment is the desire for it', the expectation that one could really do it. The *bodhicitta*, the seed of the mind's idea that it could be done — perhaps after all, it's feasible — and this, of course, takes the faithful mind. The way of faith is always an integrated, single way. Whereas, the way of wisdom is always a highly differentiated, capricious way.

His fifth reason was to show expedient means, or skillful means. In Sanskrit, it's called, **upaya kaushalya** — 'skillful means', knowing how to do it. The Greeks would have used the word **techne** — 'being technical about it', knowing how to actually, specifically, do something, and redo it every time. In other words, there is a *techne*, or a technological approach, skillful means, *upaya kaushalya*, to spiritual growth. It isn't happenstance. It works exactly. It can be taught. It can be learned. So, the fifth reason was,

---

[12] Ibid.

to show them expedient means (*upaya*) by which they may wipe away the hindrance of evil karma, guard their minds well, free themselves from stupidity and arrogance, and escape from the net of heresy.[13]

His sixth reason was,

to reveal to them the practice [of two methods of meditation], cessation [of illusions] and clear observation (*samatha* and *vipasyana*; Chinese, *chih-kuan*), so that ordinary men and the followers of Hinayana may cure their minds of error.[14]

So, cessation and clear observation. The two practices braid together and form unity. They, in fact, form the path of faith.

His seventh reason was,

to explain to them the expedient means of single-minded meditation (*smriti*) so that they may be born in the presence of the Buddha and keep their minds fixed in an unretrogressive faith.[15]

His final reason, the eighth, was,

to point out to them the advantages of [studying this treatise] and to encourage them to make an effort [to attain enlightenment].[16]

---

[13] Hakeda (1967), p. 26; Hakeda (2005), p. 5.
[14] Ibid.
[15] Hakeda (1967), p. 26; Hakeda (2005), p. 5-6.
[16] Hakeda (1967), p. 26; Hakeda (2005), p. 6.

So, those were the eight reasons that Ashvaghosha lists in the beginning. As he turns from his introduction, his salutations, his reasons for writing, he immediately becomes involved in one of the great documents of the human spiritual civilization. I've selected three paragraphs out of the work to stand as a tripod of insight for all. We have three or four translations of this, so, you can, at your own leisure, inspect the document in English.[17] There are many translations of it, but the first and the best was done incidentally by D. T. (Daisetz Teitaro) Suzuki, as a young man.[18] He was brought to a little town outside of Chicago, LaSalle, Illinois, by Dr. Paul Carus, who at that time was very much like Mr. Manly P. Hall, here at The Philosophical Research Society.[19] They were encouraging persons from all over the world to study spiritual development. They had a library there; the publishing house was called The Open Court Publishing Company. D. T. Suzuki had been picked by

---

[17]   At the time of this presentation (1982) three different translations were extant; as of December 2020, there exist four different translations of this sutra. The different versions are: (1) D. T. (Daisetz Teitaro) Suzuki, trans., *Açvaghosha's Discourse on the Awakening of Faith in the Mahayana* (Chicago: The Open Court Publishing Company, 1900), https://archive.org/details/avaghoshasdisc00asva; (2) Timothy Richard and Yang Wen Hwui, trans., *The Awakening of Faith in the Mahayana Doctrine: The New Buddhism* (Shanghai, China: Christian Literature Society, 1907), https://archive.org/details/cu31924022892198; (3a) Yoshito S. Hakeda, trans., *The Awakening of Faith* (New York: Columbia University Press, 1967); (3b) Yoshito S. Hakeda, trans., *The Awakening of Faith*, BDK English Tripitaka 63-IV (Berkeley, California: Numata Center for Buddhist Translation and Research, 2005), https://bdkamerica.org/product/the-awakening-of-faith/ (this is a reprint of the 1967 version by Hakeda); and (4) John Jorgensen et al., trans., *Treatise on Awakening Mahayana Faith* (New York: Oxford University Press, 2019).

[18]   D. T. (Daisetz Teitaro) Suzuki, trans., *Açvaghosha's Discourse on the Awakening of Faith in the Mahayana* (Chicago: The Open Court Publishing Company, 1900), https://archive.org/details/avaghoshasdisc00asva

[19]   This presentation was delivered at the Philosophical Research Society in Los Angeles, California. Weir delivered a number of presentations at the Philosophical Research Society in the 1980s.

12

his teacher, Soyen Shaku Roshi, to represent Japan at The Open Court Publishing.

When he first went from Japan to Chicago, he was asked by his instructor to make sure that he had had his own first spiritual experience of depth. D. T. Suzuki said that he struggled and struggled, and the time got closer and closer, and he was unable to make his way. He felt that he had still not had an in-depth spiritual experience. So, he made a pact with himself that he would either, in three days, have that experience, or he would do away with himself. And of course, when given these conditions, the mind cooperates. On the third day, in the eleventh hour, he had his experience. His first experience, as he would phrase it and did phrase it in his memoirs of *Satori*, he said, walking out of the little **Zendo** with his sandals on, he said for the first time he could see that all the trees were transparent. Then he noted that he was transparent, too.[20] And so, his teacher let him come to the United States, to Chicago, to LaSalle, and one of the first things he translated was Ashvaghosha's *Awakening of Faith in the Mahayana*. That was about the turn of the century.[21]

So, I have chosen three paragraphs from Ashvaghosha's work to give you an idea of the direction and movement of this seminal work. This work is the work upon which the notion of the *bodhisattva* first finds a coherent expression. In the first paragraph, he's writing about the mind in terms of phenomena, that the mind has

---

[20] "I remember that night as I walked back from the monastery to my quarters in the Kigenin temple, seeing the trees in the moonlight. They looked transparent and I was transparent too." D. T. (Daisetz Teitaro) Suzuki, The Training of the Zen Buddhist Monk (New York: University Books, 1965), p. xxii.

[21] Suzuki's translation was published in 1900.

a phenomenal occurrence. As Alfred North Whitehead would say, there are processes and events, not things and rules.[22] And the mind is an event within a phenomenal process — nothing less and nothing more than that.

Ashvaghosha writes "The mind as phenomena is grounded on...what is called the storehouse consciousness."[23] In Sanskrit, it's called the *alaya-vijnana*, the storehouse consciousness, that is, the interface between neither birth nor death, which we would call in Buddhist terms, *nirvana*. That which is neither birth nor death interfaces harmoniously with birth and death. So that *nirvana*, neither birth nor death, interfaces harmoniously with *samsara*, birth and death. So that the world of illusion and the world of beyond illusion interface and harmonize and produce a phenomenon as the storehouse consciousness, the *alaya-vijnana*, and the mind is a product of this.

> This consciousness has two aspects, which embrace all states of existence and create all states of existence. They are (1) the aspect of enlightenment, and (2) the aspect of non-enlightenment.[24]

---

[22] Alfred North Whitehead was a mathematician and philosopher who is credited with the founding of 'process philosophy'. This philosophy is based on the belief that reality consists of processes rather than material objects, and that processes are best defined by their relations with other processes, thus rejecting the theory that reality is fundamentally constructed by bits of matter that exist independently of one another.

[23] Hakeda (1967), p. 36; Hakeda (2005), p. 16.

[24] Hakeda (1967), p. 36-37; Hakeda (2005), p. 16.

So that, out of all the universe of possibilities, there are only two directions and purposes available out of this harmonious interfacing. One may either go towards birth and death — limitless; or, one may go towards enlightenment — unlimited. Those are the only two possibilities; they're the only two interfaces. But, there is such a complete confusion within the world of *samsara* that it seems that the thought of enlightenment must be the most difficult, arcane, esoteric act of all. But, in fact, it is the natural complement, always occurring without any real effort at all, to the world of *samsara*. That is the first paragraph from Ashvaghosha.

The second paragraph is the beginning statement on the practice of cessation. And remember, this was written about 78 CE. Kanishka had taken Ashvaghosha from Patna, he had taken him all the way across India, to Peshawar. There, to pride himself on his trophy, he convened the Fourth Buddhist Council. Now, the First Buddhist Council had been convened about a hundred years after the Buddha.[25] They had brought together a number of monks, and they had decided that since they were beginning to be the second and third, and perhaps even the fourth generation from the experience, that they had better bring together all of the writings that they could remember, and maybe jot them down a little bit. Just after the Buddha's **parinirvana**, there had been a gathering of monks under the senior monks, **Mahakashyapa**, and so forth.[26] And so, a hundred years later, they'd brought them together.

---

[25] The First Buddhist Council is said to have been presided over by Mahakashyapa and it is said to have been held just after Buddha's *parinirvana* (Wikipedia).

[26] Originally Weir stated 'Kashyapa', however in order to distinguish Kashyapa — the Vedic Sage — from Mahakashyapa — a principal disciple of Gautama Buddha — the editors have changed it to 'Mahakashyapa'.

Figure 5. Statue of Alexander the Great *(Macedonian Equestrian Revolutionary)* by Valentina Karanfilova-Stovanovska in Skopje, Macedonia. (Photograph by Jacqueline Schmid, Pixabay).

In the time of another great king, named **Ashoka**, there had been the Third Buddhist Council.[27] Now, Ashoka had been influenced by Alexander the Great. Ashoka's family were the Mauryas, a royal family. Under Ashoka's father, **Chandragupta Maurya**, they had witnessed the incursion of Alexander the Great's army into Northern India. In fact, not far from Peshawar, at a place called Takshasila (called today, Taxila), and there, the wonderful, undefeated Greek army of Alexander camped opposite a great Indian army.

The Buddhist wise men and the Greek philosophers, and the entourage of Alexander had a perfectly wonderful conversation through interpreters. Alexander, who was possessed by the cosmic vision of the *ecumene*, 'the one world', realized that there was a meeting of the spirits there. There was no need to force his armies farther into India. In fact, they went South, on the Indus river, and back on a great pilgrimage through the Southern desert regions to Babylon, where Alexander died.

The incursion of Alexander and his idea of a single world, the *ecumene*, his idea that man can be raised to a God-man, that human capacities are universal, not only for organization and the larger, external exoteric way, but the esoteric also, that the individual can be raised to a cosmic universal level penetrated the original Buddhism. The original doctrines in India, and the next generation began to create for themselves an empire called the **Mauryan** empire. Ashoka inherited it from his father, Chandragupta, and it extended over most of the India of that day. Only the southern tip and Ceylon

---

[27] There are records of several possible Third Buddhist Councils, however there is consensus amongst the accounts that it took place at Pataliputra during the reign of Ashoka (Wikipedia).

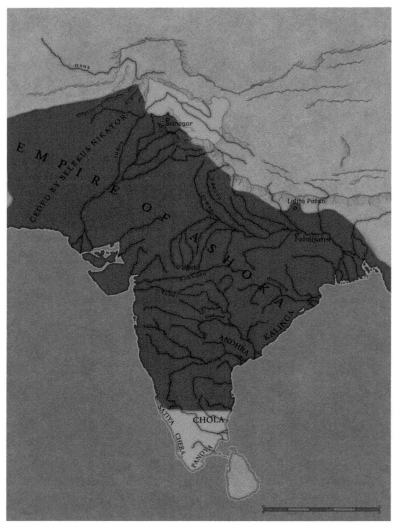

Figure 6. Empire of Ashoka circa 268 to 232 BCE. Map art by Vojtěch Burian, 2020.

were not included. All of what is today Burma, Afghanistan, and Northern India, right up to the Pamir Mountains, was included.

In other words, Ashoka had made a pattern, a template of an empire mirrored on Alexander's Greek empire. Kanishka, 300 years later, had come back and filled that template again and extended it again. When he extended the empire again on Ashoka's template, he also extended the religious ecumenicalism of Ashoka, thus, he convened the Fourth Buddhist Council at Peshawar.[28] It was a shock to many of the Southern Buddhists, they assumed that there would always be the tradition of the elders, that there would always be the disciples. One apprenticed oneself as a novice, went through the monastic communities, took their place, and in turn trained novices and disciples — and so on throughout history.

So, the convening of the Fourth Buddhist Council by Kanishka was countered by the Southern Buddhists in Sri Lanka in Ceylon, and they convened the Fourth Buddhist Council and split the Buddhist religion in two. The old path, the **Theravada**, 'The Way of the Elders', became distinct from then on, from the tradition of the so-called, in their terms, heretical sect of the Northern Buddhists.

Of course, those under Ashvaghosha, saw that they were transforming the essential message from the discipleship to the universal message of all sentient beings — whether they are here in this world, or in another world, or in another star system, or in another form other than the human form — all sentient beings no matter

---

[28] There were two "Fourth Buddhist Councils": one for the Theravada community and another for the Sarvastivada community (recognized by the Mahayana tradition). The Fourth Buddhist Council held in the Sarvastivada tradition was convened by Kanishka, the Kushan emperor (Wikipedia).

where they take rise and manifestation in the entire cosmos. The Buddhist term in the Mahayana is **chiliocosm** and sometimes **trichiliocosm**. This means 'the vast enormity of time-space that is beyond any comprehension'.

In fact, just to note here, the lifetime span of a *bodhisattva* was said at that time to be three **kalpas**. This is a time cycle that allowed for an entire manifestation of a life form process to complete its entire spectrum and go from the amoeba all the way to the highest form, man if it is, and fall into disillusion and then come back. All this would be a *kalpa*. A *bodhisattva's* lifetime is three of these enormous *kalpas* — so, they were five billion-year beings.

This enormity of mind put off and staggered the Southern Buddhist community, and they retreated into making sure that the ancient canon was preserved. So, all the Sanskrit originals were, at that time, translated into **Pali**. Pali being the language of Sri Lanka (Ceylon, at the time). It's sort of Sanskrit, with a Southern accent. Instead of Dharma, they say Damma — that sort of thing. Instead of Sutra, they say Sutta. So, all the manuscripts were translated into Pali about that time, and in fact, many of the originals that we have are not in Sanskrit — they were lost in the vicissitudes of history — but the old Pali canon is still preserved intact. We have it, almost all of it, and in the original.

This Fourth Buddhist Council was convened by Kanishka on behalf of Ashvaghosha and his Mahayana seed message. The next two paragraphs are from the basic practices, which the two of them intertwined together made the straight and true way, according to

Ashvaghosha in the 1st century CE The first was the practice of 'cessation'; the second, the practice of 'clear observation'. He wrote,

Should there be a man who desires to practice 'cessation', he should stay in a quiet place and sit erect in an even temper. [His attention should be focused] neither on breathing, nor on any form, nor on any color, nor on empty space, earth, water, fire, wind, nor even on what has been seen, heard, remembered, or conceived. All thoughts, as soon as they are conjured up, are to be discarded, and even the thought of discarding them is to be put away, for all things are essentially [in the state of] transcending thoughts, and are not to be created from moment to moment, nor to be extinguished from moment to moment; [thus one is to conform to the essential nature of Reality (*dharmata*) through this practice of cessation]. And it is not that he should first meditate on the objects of the senses in the external world and then negate them with his mind, the mind that has meditated on them. If the mind wanders away, it should be brought back and fixed in 'correct thought'. It should be understood that this 'correct thought' is [the thought that] whatever is, is mind only and that there is no external world of objects [as conceived]; even this mind is devoid of any marks of its own [which would indicate its substantiality] and therefore is not substantially conceivable as such at any moment.[29]

---

[29] Hakeda (1967), p. 96; Hakeda (2005), p. 75.

The mind and its world exists only as long as we continue to be blinded by the sheen of its imagery. As long as we continue to use our intuition to piece together the glints of the sheen of the mind's activities, we create a world, and any thought, which comes into this net and manifests itself, participates in this net. Whether it's thoughts for or against; or conversely, any kind of logical manipulation of the mind's processes, will be included in the net. So, Ashvaghosha urges us to have the practice of cessation. Let's experience what actually happens in reality without the mind.

The second and related process was the practice of 'clear observation'. This is much related to the science of our day. The Greek word for science was **episteme**, and *episteme* is the root of epistemology — 'the study of knowing'. That science is the study of how we know. What do we know? We can apply it to the world of physics, or chemistry, or biology, or space technology, whatever it is. *Episteme* is the knowing and the core of it, East and West, the practice of clear observation. What is it exactly, really? Where does it come from? Where does it go? And what does it do in between? The practice of clear observation goes with the practice of cessation, according to Ashvaghosha about 1,900 years ago.

> He who practices 'clear observation' should observe that all conditioned phenomena in the world are unstationary and are subject to an instantaneous transformation.[30]

All phenomena are subject to instantaneous transformation. It can happen at any time. There's a sense that every atomic and

---

[30] Hakeda (1967), p. 100; Hakeda (2005), p. 78.

subatomic wavelet particle phenomena transforms instantly at any time. This includes destruction, as they also pass out of materiality. All activities of the mind arise and are extinguished from moment to moment. Therefore, all of these induce suffering because of the piecing together of a tale of the world, because of the fitting together of the puzzle of illusion, and getting involved in extending those pieces in that puzzle. Of those arguments, and those desires, and purposes from that ignorance, comes the world. It all dissolves and falls apart because the connections, the interrelations, from moment to moment, are fictitious.

Ashvaghosha says they are all,

subject to instantaneous transformation and destruction; that all activities of the mind arise and are extinguished from moment to moment; and that therefore all these induce suffering. He should observe that all that had been conceived in the past [was as hazy as a dream, that all that is being conceived] in the present is like a flash of lightning,and that all that will be conceived in the future will be like clouds that rise up suddenly. He should also observe that the physical existences of all living beings in the world are impure and that among these various filthy things there is not a single one that can be sought after with joy.[31]

Not that the grain of what is, is not beautiful, not that the gown of the bodhisattva is not colorful; it is 'filthy' in the sense that it is impure, because it is unreal. It does not hold up. It transforms

---

[31] Ibid.

instantaneously, is brought into existence and destroyed. It is a constantly seething, moving morass.

This was in the 1st century CE This was the beginning of the direction of the birth of the idea of the Mahayana — 'The Great Vehicle'. The protagonists in this great vehicle were the bodhisattvas. The bodhisattvas were the enlightenment beings — those persons who had forgone their own enlightenment until all other sentient beings should be enlightened, no matter how long it took in terms of the material, phenomenal time-space. It actually took no time at all in terms of reality. The bodhisattva was not a person and individual as an egotistical phenomenon, or even a self-phenomenon, or even a not self-phenomenon had transcended all of these polarities and particularly particular peculiarities at the same time. It had compassion for all, individually. The notion of the bodhisattva in the Mahayana was, from the beginning, full of contradictions that were never hidden. They were always posted side by side, always left clearly expressed. That one had no clear individuality and yet revered all clear individuality. That one had the capacity for universal enlightenment and would not go through with it until all had this.

These contradictory ideas — on the material, phenomenal plane — were held in perfect sympathy. At the time of Ashvaghosha, there began then to be a generation of persons who were not in the monastic orders, who were lay persons, much like ourselves.

PART II
THE VIMALAKIRTI SUTRA

One of the most famous of the Mahayana sutras, called the **Vimalakirti Sutra**,[32] was written within a generation of Ashvaghosha, about 110, 120, or 130 CE — the time of Trajan, or Hadrian, in the Roman empire, about the same time as Tacitus' *Histories*, about the time that Justin Martyr would have been writing in Rome.

---

[32] Generally known as the *Vimalakirtinirdesa Sutra*, there are five different English translations of this text: (1) Robert A. F. Thurman, trans., *The Holy Teaching of Vimalakirti: A Mahayana Scripture* (University Park, Pennsylvania: The Pennsylvania State University Press, 1976); (2) Sara Boin and Etienne Lamotte, trans., *The Teaching of Vimalakirti (Vimalakirtinirdesa)*, Sacred Books of the Buddhists 32 (London: The Pali Text Society, 1976); (3) Charles Luk, trans., *The Vimalakirti Nirdesa Sutra* (Boston: Shambhala Publications, 1990); (4) Burton Watson, trans., *The Vimalakirti Sutra* (New York: Columbia University Press, 1997); and (5) John R. McRae, trans., "The *Vimalakirti Sutra*," in *The Sutra of Queen Srimala of the Lion's Roar: The Vimalakirti Sutra*, BDK English Tripitaka 26-I (Berkeley, California: Numata Center for Buddhist Translation and Research, 2004), p. 63-201, https://bdkamerica.org/product/the-sutra-of-queen-srimala-of-the-lions-roar-and-the-vimalakirti-sutra/. According to Buddhist scholar Jan Nattier, out of the four translations published prior to 2000, the Thurman translation is the truest to the original text (see Jan Nattier, "The Teaching of Vimalkirti (Vimalakirtinirdesa): A Review of Four English Translations," *Buddhist Literature* 2 (2000): 234-58, http://www.shin-ibs.edu/documents/BL2/04Nattier.pdf).

Figure 7. A cave painting from the Tang Dynasty depicting a scene from the *Vimalakirtinirdesa Sutra. (Manjushri Bodhisattva Debates Vimalakirti,* Mogao Caves, Dunhuang, China; photograph by Flickr user pandahermit).

Figure 8. A cave painting from the Tang Dynasty depicting a scene from the Vimalakirtinirdesa Sutra. (*Vimalakirti Debates Manjushri Bodhisattva,* Mogao Caves, Dunhuang, China; photograph by Flickr user pandahermit).

The *Vimalakirti Sutra* has, as its central hero, protagonist, not a monk but a layman. In fact, the layman, whose name is **Yuima**,[33] is portrayed in startling contrast to the monks, including some of the most famous monks and some of the great transcendental beings of the time. It's an interesting story. In the *Vimalakirti Sutra*, Yuima has suddenly taken ill. He is indisposed. The Buddha, hearing of this, for the Sutra assumes that this happened in the Buddha's time, decides he would like to know how Yuima is doing. So, he goes and inquires after Yuima. The monk says, "Honorable one, I beg not to be sent." The Buddha says, "Why is this?" And he says, "I've been to see Yuima. We always get into discussions, and I always lose."

And the practice at that time, of course, was that when you lost a philosophical discussion with someone, a religious philosophical discussion, you became their student, and that person became your master. This was the old **Upanishadic** Sanskrit way.

So, the Buddha finally turns to his chief disciple, a man named **Sariputra**. And he says, "Sariputra, I think that you should go see Yuima." And Sariputra says, "Why not send Mahakashyapa? He's the oldest of us all." So, the Buddha says, "Well, Mahakashyapa, will you go?" Mahakashyapa says, "I-I really can't go." And the Buddha says, "Well, I'll have to hear your story. Why can't you go see this poor, sick layman?" Mahakashyapa replies, "Sir, once I was there with my begging bowl and as I was having my begging bowl filled across the way, Yuima, who was a very rich man, stepped across the street and chastised me for accepting food from only the poor. He said, 'Why are you always taking from the poor? They can't afford this. Whereas the rich can afford it much better. And besides,

---

[33] Yuima is the Japanese name for Vimalakirti.

there's a hidden egotism here. You're thinking that you're giving the poor a chance for charity, and you're setting yourself superior to them. You're really making yourself very, very fancy underneath it all by accepting the food from the poor'." Mahakashyapa says, "By the time I was through, I almost left my begging bowl on the curb. I couldn't stand to eat the food." So, the Buddha says, "Very well, we'll send someone else."

So, he picked his most subtle disciple named **Subhuti**. And he says, "Subhuti, you go and check on Yuima." And Subhuti says, "Honorable sir, I'm-I'm terribly sorry, but I have a very similar predicament as Mahakashyapa. I was there with my begging bowl, and Yuima finally convinced me that all things were just phantom existences, and that everything was just names really. And that, in fact, one day we had to go beyond the arrangement of names, beyond the normal logic of discourse, which we were even involved in at that time, the very thing to a sense of reality. I really got alarmed with what I was beginning to intuit. And I would rather not go."

And so, the Buddha, looking up and raising himself, addresses himself to the future Buddha, **Maitreya**. He says, "Will you go to interview this layman?" And by this time, of course, it became a cause célèbre." And Maitreya, in the **Tushita** heaven discoursing on the life of non-retrogression, apologizes. He says, "Even I cannot go see this layman. This layman is unbelievable. He's unbeatable. And he even appeared once here in the Tushita heaven, and we had a discourse. And he prophesied that you, **Shakyamuni**, would have enlightenment in just one lifetime. And he asked me, 'Would I have enlightenment in just one lifetime? And was that lifetime a past lifetime? Because if it was so, it's past, it's gone. Would it be a future lifetime, that is not yet manifest? Is it the present lifetime? And what in the present lifetime has substantiality to allow for you to exist to have enlightenment?'" And he says, "By the time, I was through. I was a little shaken myself."

That poor Yuima! No one to visit him to see how his health was. Finally, the great bodhisattva of wisdom, **Manjushri**, agreed to go. He collected among his entourage this group of 8,000 bodhisattvas and 500 *sravakas*, or disciples, and 200,000 **deva** lords. And this enormous cosmic entourage descended with Manjushri to the sick layman, Yuima. And Yuima had cleared out his house and had positioned himself in just his bedroom. In fact, the bedroom had been cleared out. And there was just one couch in there, upon which Yuima lay sick. And among the *sravakas* was Subhuti to see how Manjushri was going to handle this. So, Manjushri comes in, and Yuima looks up and says, "Oh Manjushri, you are welcome indeed, but your coming is no coming, and my seeing is no seeing." And Manjushri replies, "You are right. You are quite right. I come as if not coming. I depart as if not departing. For my coming is from nowhere, and my departing is no wither. We talk of seeing each other, and yet there is no seeing between us two, but let us put this matter aside for a while, for I am here commissioned by the Buddha to inquire after your condition. Is it improving? How did you become ill? Are you cured?"

Yuima, looking up from his couch, quite interested, says, "From folly, there is no desire, and this is the cause of my illness because all sentient beings are sick. I am sick, and when they are all cured of illnesses, I will be cured of my illness. A bodhisattva must assume a life of birth and death, a life in *samsara* for the sake of all beings. And as long as there is still birth and death, then there is my illness." And, of course, this is the great doctrine of the bodhisattvas transposed in one generation, from the brilliancy of a single monk, Ashvaghosha, to the personage of a layman completely outside of that tradition.

In fact, we notice in the *Vimalakirti Sutra*, the first indication that those who were disciples in a strict, close-minded lineage order were exempt from even understanding what the world of reality was about. That there had been this transformation. That the achievement of a certain level of capacity had transformed the entire universe, and that it was different. And those who had learned an old way before were indeed lost and baffled because everything was anew. Nothing had stayed the same. All transforms instantaneously. All passes in and out of existence. And we cannot cling even to the truth of the past but must forever see it clearly anew.

So, Sariputra, who was the chief disciple of the Buddha, wonders how all this entourage is going to get into this 10-foot square, bare room. "Where are the chairs?" he says. Yuima, hearing Sariputra murmur this, says, "Did you come for the Dharma, or did you come for a seat?" And Sariputra is kind of embarrassed. He says, "Well, I came for the Dharma, of course." Yuima says, "Well, seeking the Dharma consists of not seeking anything. Not getting attached. Not having hindrances. Not engendering contradictions or altercations. So, let us ask Manjushri where we can get the best chairs." Manjushri replies, "Well, there is a Buddha land way out over there where we can get the finest chairs." So, they bring in 32,000 chairs to Yuima's little 10-foot square, barren room, and all of them are elaborate and ornamented, high and broad, fit for any august bodhisattva. All 8,000 of them come in to take their places, to be seated, and the 200,000 deva lords come in. Sariputra is absolutely worried; he says, "I just don't know." This chair is shown to him, and of course, it's too high. He can't climb up into it, and so, he is staggered by this.

So, Sariputra, realizing how small the room is where this entire crowd is asked to sit, wonders how it can be done. As he's wondering that, as that thought occurs to him, as the thought of the contradiction of what is transpiring in the Mahayana occurs to that one greatly attained in the old way, he notices that there is a celestial maiden who is causing flowers to be showered and sprinkled and rained inside the room. All the wonderful assemblage there, the 8,000 bodhisattvas, are sitting on their beautiful, high, ornate chairs, and the flowers are just falling off them. And they're raining down.

Sariputra looks, and the flowers are sticking to him and he's trying to brush them off. The other *sravakas*, or disciples, are trying to brush these flowers off. They're sticking to him, and he begins to talk to the goddess. She says to him, "Why? Why do you wish to brush these flowers off you?" And Sariputra replies, "Well, this is not in accordance with the dignity of the Dharma." She says, "Don't say so. These flowers are free from discrimination. That is why they are falling off the bodhisattvas, but they are clinging to you. These are wonderful flowers. These are cosmic flowers raining down, blessing this situation. And here you are complaining, and they're sticking to you because these are free from discrimination." So, Sariputra responds, "How long have you been in this room?" And she says, "As long as the length of your own emancipation."

This is the first appearance of our goddess Kuan Yin — the gorgeous celestial maiden who rains the flowers of compassion down upon all beings in the phenomenal world. They, being the blossoms of non-discrimination, free from it, are able to cascade beautifully and pass through the phenomenal existence.

Yuima then begins to have the end of the conversation in the sutra with Manjushri. After this nice little talk between Sariputra and the celestial goddess, the sutra comes back, and all this time, Sariputra and Manjushri have been talking about universal, cosmic design. They have talked about a phrase, which includes the Sanskrit word *advaita*, non-duality. They have discussed how the world of reality is neither dual nor non-dual, that it transcends these categories, these capacities. Manjushri, in great homage, has explained this wonderful doctrine and then asks Yuima, "Do you agree?" Yuima remains silent. Manjushri beams in great joy and says, "Well done, Yuima, well done. Your silence has shown that you understand."

Then Sariputra, who is by now completely out of the conversation, doesn't understand Yuima's silence. He doesn't understand the transpiring dialogue, he just suddenly notices that he's hungry. Yuima, looking up, says to Sariputra, "Food will be served to all. In fact, we have scouted the universe, and we have the most succulent, delectable meals for everyone." Sariputra, wondering how all these bodhisattvas and devas and so forth could be seated, now wonders how they could all be fed.

And in this confusion of the old way, the *Vimalakirti Sutra* ends with all of the assembled Mahayana hosts sampling an infinitely infinitesimal amount of nourishment that is not even physically there. It is just referred to in the terms of, from the fragrant Buddha land. The fragrance and the odor of the food, which is not there, wafts through this assemblage of the great Mahayana masters and passes on.

Thus, the *Vimalakirti Sutra*, followed very closely on the heels of the *Shraddhotpada Mahayana Sutra* [*Awakening of Faith in the Mahayana*], and this penetration of the idea that enlightenment had transcended the old tradition. It had completely broken the bounds of form that had been given to it in the past. It had been venerated for 500 or 600 years, perhaps even close to 700 years, and suddenly opened up. The doctrine of *tathata*, of suchness, was joined by a doctrine of that which transcends all polarities, that which no longer participates in the normal, polarized world phenomenon, but is in a reality beyond. This reality beyond is born from the swollenness of the illusion of phenomenal existence. Out of that swollenness, the inside of that is hollow. So that, the complement to the swollen illusion of the universe being something, or perhaps not something, inside was the hollow emptiness called, in Sanskrit, **shunyata**. Thus, *shunyata* and *tathata* were brought together. The one from the practice of cessation, to see reality as it was in its suchness, and the practice of clear observation to see that there was emptiness beyond all polarized, phenomenal, or noumenal concepts, and that the emptiness and the suchness were brought together and braided together.

This path, so difficult to conceive because it was not conceivable, so difficult to follow because it didn't lead anywhere, because it didn't come from any wither, was promulgated about the 2nd century CE and brought together by one of the great minds of civilization. That man's name was Nagarjuna.

Nagarjuna was responsible for the introduction of the concept of zero into mathematics. Without zero, there is no tenable viable mathematical structure, and, in fact, the *shunyata* of the Buddhists of that time later on became introduced and known. I think that the Arabic word for it was *sifr*, out of which we get the Latin *cipher*, which means 'the not', 'the zero'. It was only about the time that they were building the Gothic cathedrals, about the middle of the 12th century, that the notion of the *cipher* penetrated fully into Western, Latin-speaking Europe.

This 'not', this *shunyata*, this emptiness, combined with the suchness of the *tathata*, brought together the two possibilities that make up the character of the bodhisattva — that enlightenment being who embodies, beyond time-space, the wisdom of emptiness and the compassion of suchness. Also, because it is not limited by any contradictoriness on any logical, plain realm whatsoever, penetrates through as a helper for a man who is trapped in the illusion of the net of his own mental worlds. These helpers bring the nourishment, the milky opalescent nectar, to the young man in his bubble, which will allow him to sound the gracefulness in resonance of his own being to burst that bubble and be born into freedom and reality, and to join the worlds of the bodhisattvas.

This notion developed and grew, and very soon, there was a movement afoot that there must be a place, a realm, a Buddha land, a Western paradise, wherein man, born from the bubble and freed from his illusion, can then learn all of the exacting details by correct observation, clear observation, and by the practice of cessation, where he can piece together the world as it really is. This Western paradise, called *Sukavati*, in Sanskrit, became the home of the **Amida Buddha** — the Buddha who radiates a golden light through time-space. The whole phenomenon of the Amida Buddha and his emanation of the great bodhisattva of Kuan Yin, Kannon in Japan, becomes the helper for human beings who are freed from the bubble of illusion, but yet have to learn all of the details of the natural world. Those are the two tasks that are needed; not just the perception of suchness, things as they are, but the understanding of all relationalities through wisdom. When man is born out of his bubble world into the cosmos as a totality in a whole, it is only then that he can begin to go to school for the very first time.

Figure 9. Amitabha Buddha residing in the pureland of Sukhavati with the 8 great bodhisattvas seated at the sides. *Buddha Amitabha in His Pure Land of Suvakti,* Central Tibet, 18th century, ground mineral pigment on cotton, Rubin Museum of Art. (Wikimedia Commons).

PART III
THE ACCUMULATION OF PRECIOUS QUALITIES

All of the scrolls of the **Amitabha Buddha**, all of the compli-
cated worlds which are expressed there, show people on every level
studying, reading, listening to discourses, putting together all of the
detailing. So that, the paradise of the Amitabha Buddha is not one
of just singing and mindlessness, but one of study and great erudition because the bodhisattva ideal includes omniscience — one must
know it all — every bit of it, in all of its ramifications, for all beings
to learn. These, in fact, are called 'The Precious Qualities'. I have
here a couple of lines from a work called, ***The Accumulation of
Precious Qualities [Prajna-paramita-ratna-guna-samcaya-
gatha]***,[34] to give the universal application of this:

---

[34] The only English translation of this text is by Edward Conze. He published
an initial version in 1962 and a second, extended version in 1973. Edward
Conze, "The Accumulation of Precious Qualities *(Prajna paramita ratna guna
samcaya gatha),*" *Indo-Asian Studies* Part 1 (1962): 125-78; Edward Conze, *The
Perfection of Wisdom in Eight Thousand Lines and Its Verse Summary,* Wheel
Series 1 (Bolinas, California: Four Seasons Foundation, 1973), https://archive.org/
details/perfectionofwisdomineightthousandlinesedwardconze_502_w/. See entry
for "*Prajna-paramita-ratna-guna-samcaya-gatha (The Accumulation of Precious
Qualities)*" in the Key Terms section.

Forms are not wisdom nor is wisdom found in form,
In consciousness, perceptions, feeling, or in will.
They are not wisdom, and no wisdom is in them.
Like space it is, without a break or crack.[35]

In other words, infinite universal space is the only metaphor that we could have to give us an idea of what reality actually is. Later on, there is a 'simile of the cosmos' in *The Accumulation of Precious Qualities.* This is a bodhisattva argument, and it runs like this:

Supported by space is air and (by that) the mass of water; by that again is supported this great Earth and the living world. If the foundation of the enjoyment of the deeds of beings is thus established in space, how can one think of that object? Just so the bodhisattva, who is established in emptiness manifests manifold and various works to beings in the world, and his vows and cognitions are a force which sustains beings. But he does not experience the Blessed Rest; for emptiness is not a place to stand on. At the time when the wise and learned bodhisattva courses in this most excellent quietude of the concentration on emptiness, during that time no sign should be exalted. Nor should he stand in the signless; for he is one who courses calm and quiet beyond signs and beyond the signless.[36]

---

[35] Edward Conze, "The Accumulation of Precious Qualities *(Prajna paramita ratna guna samcaya gatha),"* p. 132; Edward Conze, *The Perfection of Wisdom in Eight Thousand Lines and Its Verse Summary,* p. 14.

[36] Edward Conze, "The Accumulation of Precious Qualities *(Prajna paramita ratna guna samcaya gatha),"* p. 152-53; Edward Conze, *The Perfection of Wisdom in Eight Thousand Lines and Its Verse Summary,* p. 45-46.

Figure 10. Artist rendering of the Milky Way galaxy (Image by NASA/JPL-Caltech).

Figure 11. Artist rendering of the Andromeda galaxy (Image by NASA/JPL-CalTech).

Figure 12. Artist rendering of the Large Magellanic Clouds dwarf galaxy (Image by NASA).

PART IV
THE SPACE AGE

This, of course, brings us closer to the imagery of our time —
the imagery of man freeing himself from what he considers to be
the fetters of the world in a technological mode, freeing himself to
explore and expand. As he does so, he finds himself, increasingly,
through the 1970s and now into the 1980s, faced with a conundrum,
which has begun to occur again and again to sensitive beings.[37] It
is one thing by the stretch of egotistical power to extend man into
an orbit around the Earth — that can be done and has been done.
Or, even to push a material phenomenal time-space-being to the
moon — and that has been done. It's incapacitated to make that far
of a leap spiritually from the Earth, and in fact, we see more and
more that man is raising himself up on his tiptoes only, and still
constrained, because he still operates under the illusion that this
is a universe of time and space, of force and power. However, that
seems to not be the case.

In fact, it seems to be more the flow of process and event of a
transcendental spirituality. As we burst the bubble that had surrounded us, and we find ourselves freed from that illusion, it is

---

[37] This presentation was delivered in 1982.

only then that we can begin to study and expand ourselves. Only then, we realize the old expressions in the earliest writings of the Mahayana — which are actually contemporaneous with the same development, which was reflected in Alexandria in the West (which came about the very same time as Ashoka's empire), or represented in its manifestation in the West, because the early gospels are exactly contemporaneous with Ashvaghosha, that all of these ideas are not alien at all to any beings on the surface of the globe.

When we begin to expand our sense of phenomenal time-space, we experience that giddiness of the mind, which shows that its capacities are no longer operative; that it has finally come into a realm where the sheen of the inner surface of the bubble no longer makes a continuity. Whether it's the vicissitudes of the particles and wave phenomena of the inner atomic structure, or the expanding vision of what size the universe is, we realize that we are able to envision our sun as a grapefruit-sized object, and that the nearest star is about Denver, Colorado.[38] Several hundred million stars make one huge wheel — our Milky Way Galaxy — which is 200,000 light-years across.[39] That's just one part of a group of island universes including the Andromeda and the Magellanic Clouds. That's just one particle in this enormous gulf between even those groupings of island universes. So that we could, just a few years ago, make a map — not of stars but of galaxies. On the Harvard map of galax-

---

[38] Weir is using an example to illustrate the scale of the universe — that a grapefruit-sized object in Los Angeles, California and an object located in Denver, Colorado are, relatively speaking, similar distances as our sun and the nearest star.

[39] Weir originally stated, "Several hundred million stars make one huge wheel, which takes 200,000 light years to make a revolution." The editors have revised this to reflect the diameter instead of the revolution or orbit of the Milky Way Galaxy.

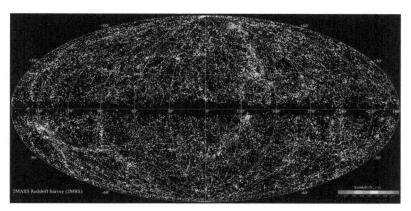

Figure 13. An illustration showing the results from the Two-Micron All-SkySurvey (2MASS) conducted by Harvard-Smithsonian astrophysicists to map galaxies in the universe. The plane of the Milky Way runs horizontally across the center of the image. The image depicts more than 43,000 galaxies within 380 million light-years from Earth. (Illustration by T. H. Jarrett, IPAC/SSC, Harvard-Smithsonian Center for Astrophysics, 2011).

ies, there are some six million galaxies pinpointed and dotted for us. Each one of the dots of lights representing groups of island universes without end.

We begin to realize that our capacities to be deluded are finally running dry. We are finally beginning to wake up to the possibilities that there is a transcendental source of nourishment, which is universal, which encourages us, indeed, to be born from that bubble, but at the same time, encourages us to understand that through study and excellence, we may understand and participate, not in phenomenal time-space, but in reality, as it is beyond.

BIBLIOGRAPHY

Boin, Sara, and Etienne Lamotte, trans. *The Teaching of Vimalakirti (Vimalakirtinirdesa)*. Sacred Books of the Buddhists 32. London: The Pali Text Society, 1976.

Conze, Edward. *The Perfection of Wisdom in Eight Thousand Lines and Its Verse Summary*. Wheel Series 1. Bolinas, California: Four Seasons Foundation, 1973. https://archive.org/details/perfectionofwisdomineightthousandlinesedwardconze_502_w/.

Conze, Edward. *The Prajnaparamita Literature*. 2nd ed. Bibliographia Philologica Buddhica - Series Maior 1. Tokyo: The Reiyukai Library, 1978. https://sisu.ut.ee/sites/default/files/orientalistika/files/conze_e._the_prajnaparamita_literature_1978.pdf.

Conze, Edward, trans. "The Accumulation of Precious Qualities (Prajna Paramita Ratna Guna Samcaya Gatha)." *Indo-Asian Studies* Part 1 (1962): 125-78.

Edgerton, Franklin. "The Prajna-Paramita-Ratna-Guna-Samcaya-Gatha." *Indo-Iranian Journal* 5, no. 1 (1961): 1-18. http://www.jstor.org/stable/24646838.

Hakeda, Yoshito S., trans. *The Awakening of Faith.* New York: Columbia University Press, 1967.

Hakeda, Yoshito S., trans. *The Awakening of Faith.* BDK English Tripitaka 63-IV. Berkeley, California: Numata Center for Buddhist Translation and Research, 2005. https://bdkamerica.org/product/the-awakening-of-faith/.

Jorgensen, John, Dan Lusthaus, John Makeham, and Mark Strange, trans. *Treatise on Awakening Mahayana Faith.* New York: Oxford University Press, 2019.

Keown, Damien. *A Dictionary of Buddhism.* New York: Oxford University Press, 2003. https://doi.org/10.1093/acref/9780198605607.001.0001.

Luk, Charles, trans. *The Vimalakirti Nirdesa Sutra.* Boston: Shambhala Publications, 1990.

McRae, John R., trans. "The Vimalakirti Sutra." In *The Sutra of Queen Srimala of the Lion's Roar; The Vimalakirti Sutra,* 63-201. BDK English Tripitaka 26-I. Berkeley, California: Numata Center for Buddhist Translation and Research, 2004. https://bdkamerica.org/product/the-sutra-of-queen-srimala-of-the-lions-roar-and-the-vimalakirti-sutra/.

Nattier, Jan. "The Teaching of Vimalakirti (Vimalakirtinirdesa): A Review of Four English Translations." *Buddhist Literature* 2 (2000): 234-58. http://www.shin-ibs.edu/documents/BL2/04Nattier.pdf.

Obermiller, E., ed. *Prajna Paramita-Ratna-Guna-Samcaya-Gatha: Sanscrit and Tibetan Text*. Bibliotheca Buddhica 29. Osnabruck, West Germany: Biblio Verlag, 1970. https://archive.org/details/in.ernet.dli.2015.282607.

Richard, Timothy and Yang Wen Hwui, trans. *The Awakening of Faith in the Mahayana Doctrine: The New Buddhism*. Shanghai, China: Christian Literature Society, 1907. https://archive.org/details/cu31924022892198.

Suzuki, D. T. (Daisetz Teitaro), trans. *Açvaghosha's Discourse on the Awakening of Faith in the Mahayana*. Chicago: The Open Court Publishing Company, 1900. https://archive.org/details/avaghoshasdisc00asva.

Suzuki, D. T. (Daisetz Teitaro). *The Training of the Zen Buddhist Monk*. New York: University Books, 1965.

Thurman, Robert A. F., trans. *The Holy Teaching of Vimalakirti: A Mahayana Scripture*. University Park, Pennsylvania: The Pennsylvania State University Press, 1976.

Watson, Burton, trans. *The Vimalakirti Sutra*. New York: Columbia University Press, 1997. https://archive.org/details/BurtonWatsonTHEVIMALAKIRTISUTRAFromTheChineseVersionByKumarajiva.

Yuyama, Akira, ed. *Prajna-Paramita-Ratna-Guna-Samcaya-Gatha (Sanskrit Recension A)*. Cambridge: Cambridge University Press, 1976.

KEY TERMS

The following terms and phrases appear within the text and are included here in order to provide further details regarding their meaning and context. Unless otherwise noted the definitions listed below have been sourced from *A Dictionary of Buddhism* by Damien Keown.[1]

Advaita

A Sanskrit philosophical term that may be literally rendered in English as 'nonduality': denoting that though differences and variegation appear in the human condition they are unreal or illusory and are not ultimately true.[2]

Alaya-vijnana

The eighth consciousness, being the substratum or 'storehouse' consciousness according to the philosophy of the Yogacara school. The alaya-vijnana acts as the receptacle in which the impressions (known as vasana or bija) of past experience and karmic actions are stored. From it the remaining seven consciousnesses arise and produce all present and future modes of experience in

---

[1]   Damien Keown, *A Dictionary of Buddhism* (New York: Oxford University Press, 2003), https://doi.org/10.1093/acref/9780198605607.001.0001.

[2]   This definition is from Wiktionary, https://en.wiktionary.org/.

samsara. At the moment of enlightenment (bodhi), the alaya-vijnana is transformed into the Mirror-like Awareness or perfect discrimination of a Buddha.

Amida Buddha

The Japanese pronunciation of the name of the Buddha Amitabha or Amitayus. This Buddha serves as the primary object of devotion and agent of salvation for the various schools of Pure Land Buddhism in Japan, such as the Jodo Shu, the Jodo Shinshu, and the Jishu.

Amitabha Buddha

The Buddha 'Infinite Light', also known as Amitayus (Infinite Life). One of the five Jinas, he is normally depicted iconographically as a red sambhoga-kaya Buddha associated with the western quarter. He is also viewed as the embodiment of Discriminating Awareness, one of the five awarenesses, and as the lord of the Lotus Family. Early Mahayana devotion to Amitabha gave rise to a belief in his Pure Land, known as Sukhavati.

Ashoka

Grandson of Chandragupta Maurya, son of Bindusara, and third incumbent of the Mauryan throne, c.272-231 BCE. Ashoka is famous for the edicts he ordered to be carved on rocks and pillars throughout his kingdom. A total of 33 inscriptions have been found which provide invaluable historical and chronological information on early Indian Buddhist history. He was a great patron of Buddhism, and it can be seen from the Edicts that the content of Ashoka's Dharma is essentially that of a lay Buddhist. Dharma consists, he tells us, of 'Few sins and many good deeds of kindness, liberality, truthfulness and purity' (Pillar Edict 2). In his edicts Ashoka offers father-like advice to his subjects, commending moral virtues such as peacefulness, piety, religious tolerance, zeal, respect for parents and teachers, courtesy, charity, sense-control, and equanimity. No reference is made to the technical aspects of Buddhist doctrine as expounded in the Four Noble Truths. Ashoka relates in Rock Edict XIII that after his bloody conquest of the Kalinga region of north-east India, he repented of his warlike ways and became a lay Buddhist. From then on, he attempted to rule according to Dharma as a 'Dharma-raja' or righteous king. He appointed officers known as 'superintendents of Dharma' (dharma-mahamatra) to propagate the religion. However, in the best tradition of Indian kingship, Ashoka supported all religions. One of the edicts towards the end of his reign, known as the 'schism edict', condemns schism in the Sangha and speaks of monks being expelled. This seems to confirm accounts in Buddhist chronicles of his involvement in a council at Pataliputra around 250 BCE, reckoned as the 'Third Council' by the Theravada tradition. The edicts also record that Ashoka sent ambassadors to five named kings reigning in the Hellenistic world, which again seems to support the Buddhist tradition that he did much to promote the spread of the religion. He is credited with sending his son Mahinda, himself a monk, to Sri Lanka to establish Buddhism there, as well as sending missionaries to other parts of south-east Asia. After Ashoka's death in 231 BCE Mauryan rule rapidly declined and in the 2nd century BCE the north and north-west were extensively invaded by Greeks from the former Seleucid satrapies of Bactria and Parthia, as well as by central Asian nomadic tribes. Various Ashokan emblems, such as the lion capital found on his pillars, have been adopted for official use by the modern state of India.

Ashvaghosha

An early Sarvastivadin master, born 1st-2nd century CE in Ayodhya. A court poet of the Kushan king Kanishka (it is not clear whether this was Kanishka I or II), he composed poetic and dramatic works on Buddhist themes, such as the *Buddhacarita*, a life of the Buddha, the *Saundarananda*, an account of the conversion of Nanda, and the *Sariputraprakarana* or 'Story of Sariputra'. Tradition also ascribes to him the *Shraddhotpada Mahayana Sutra* (*The Awakening of Faith in the Mahayana*). His most famous work is the first of these, a biography of the Buddha in epic mahakavya style (the style of the great Sanskrit literary classics). Originally in 28 cantos, only 17 survive in Sanskrit, the remainder being preserved in Tibetan and Chinese translations. The author's deep respect and reverence for the Buddha is unmistakable in all his compositions and he is viewed by many as a follower of the Mahayana.

Bodhicitta

Sanskrit for 'thought of awakening'. A key term in Mahayana Buddhism denoting the state of mind of a bodhisattva. Two aspects are recognized: the relative aspect, or the mind (citta) of a bodhisattva directed towards enlightenment (bodhi); and the absolute aspect or the mind whose intrinsic nature is enlightenment. The former relative aspect is also said to be twofold: the bodhicitta of aspiration (pranidhana), when one announces one's intention to pursue the bodhisattva Path, and the bodhicitta of application, by which one engages in the path.

Bodhisattva

The embodiment of the spiritual ideal of Mahayana Buddhism, in contrast to the earlier Arhat ideal advocated by the Hinayana. bodhisattva literally means 'enlightenment being' but the correct Sanskrit derivation may be 'bodhi-sakta' meaning 'a being who is orientated towards enlightenment'. The ideal is inspired by the lengthy career of the Buddha before he became enlightened, as described in the *Jatakas*. A bodhisattva begins his career by generating the aspiration (pranidhana) to achieve enlightenment for the sake of all beings, often in the form of a vow, which according to many Mahayana texts is often accompanied by a prediction of success (vyakarana) by a Buddha. He then embarks on the path leading to enlightenment (bodhi) by cultivating the Six Perfections (sad-paramita) and the four means of attracting beings (samgraha-vastu) over the course of three immeasurable kalpas. The spiritual progress of a bodhisattva is usually subdivided into ten stages or levels (bhumi). Many Mahayana sutras state that a bodhisattva forgoes his own final enlightenment until all other beings in samsara have been liberated, or else describe a special form of nirvana, the unlocalized nirvana (apratistha-nirvana) by virtue of which a bodhisattva may be 'in the world but not of it'. Earlier Mahayana sutras are specific in their belief that a bodhisattva can only be male but later texts allow the possibility of female bodhisattvas.

Chandragupta Maurya

Founder of the Mauryan dynasty and grandfather of Ashoka,
Chandragupta seized power with the help of his political
adviser Canaka. He established his capital at Pataliputra and
considerably extended the territory of the previous Nanda
dynasty. He defeated the Greek general Seleucus Nikator in
305 BCE and as the result of a treaty concluded between them
in 303 territory in the north-west was ceded to the Indians.
As part of the same treaty ambassadors were exchanged and
the Greek ambassador Megasthenes took up residence at the
Mauryan capital. Chandragupta further extended his kingdom
to the south down as far as the Narmada river. After reigning
for 24 years, he was succeeded by his son Bindusara, who
continued the expansion to the south. According to legend,
Chandragupta became a Jain and went to live in south India
where he eventually starved himself to death in accordance with
Jain custom.

Chiliocosm

A collection of many worlds. Some texts adapt this traditional
Buddhist concept to modern astronomy, where the worlds are
solar systems and hence the chiliocosm is a galaxy.[3]

Deva

A god or supernatural being, normally resident in one of the
numerous heavens and reborn there as the result of good karma.
Buddhism inherited the Vedic concept of a pantheon of gods,
originally 33, but which rapidly expanded in number. The gods
are thought to reside on or over Mt. Meru, the cosmic mountain,

---

[3] Ibid.

and to be frequent visitors to the human world, especially to hear the Buddha's teachings. Offerings and sacrifices are made to the gods, and they may be appealed to for help or protection. They enjoy lifespans of hundreds of thousands of years, but are eventually reborn when their good karma is exhausted, and are thus (in contrast to the Buddha) still within the realm of samsara.

Dharma

Etymologically derived from the Sanskrit root 'dhr' meaning to bear or support, Dharma is a term of great significance with three main meanings. First, it refers to the natural order or universal law that underpins the operation of the universe in both the physical and moral spheres. Secondly, it denotes the totality of Buddhist teachings, since these are thought to accurately describe and explain the underlying universal law so that individuals may live in harmony with it. It is in this sense that it occurs as one of the 'three jewels' (triratna) and the 'three refuges' (trisarana), along with the Buddha and the Sangha. Thirdly, it is used in the Abhidharma system of taxonomy to refer to the individual elements that collectively constitute the empirical world. Some of these elements (dharmas) are external to the perceiver and others are internal psychological processes and traits of character. It is in this context that the Madhyamaka school denied the substantial reality of dharmas, claiming that all phenomena were 'empty' (sunya) of any substantial reality.

Ecumene

All known inhabited areas of the world.[4]

---

[4]   Ibid.

Episteme

Scientific knowledge; a principled system of understanding; sometimes contrasted with empiricism.[5]

Gassho

A Japanese term meaning 'to bring the palms together' as in the Indian gesture of respectful salutation known as 'anjali'. This is a gesture of respect between clerics and also a ritual gesture of worship. The term is also found in Chinese Buddhism under the Chinese pronunciation 'ho-chang'.

Kalpa

An aeon; a measurement of time widely used in ancient India. Several accounts exist of the precise number of years involved, and there are also small, medium, great, and 'uncountable' kalpas. The most common values given for an 'uncountable' (asamkhyeya) kalpa are 10^{51}, 10^{59}, or 10^{63} years. A bodhisattva is said to become a Buddha after three of these 'uncountable' kalpas.

Kanishka

The third king of the north-west and central Indian Kushan dynasty who ruled c.128-51 CE. He was renowned as a patron of Buddhism, sometimes even regarded as a 'second Ashoka', and was particularly associated with the Sarvastivada school. A council was held under his patronage at Gandhara, which led to the compilation of the *Mahavibhasa*.

---

[5]   Ibid.

Kuan Yin

(Sanskrit; Japanese form, Kannon) One form of the Chinese
name assigned to the bodhisattva of compassion (karuna),
Avalokitesvara. This Chinese form means 'to hear or regard
the sounds', and is a contraction of Kuan Shih Yin 'to hear or
regard the sounds of the world', indicating the bodhisattva's
ability to hear the cries of all beings in need or trouble. In the
Heart Sutra, he is given the name Kuan Tzu Tsai. He is one of
the most popular objects of devotion and reverence in east Asian
Buddhism. The *locus classicus* for Kuan Yin's major attributes
and functions is the seventh fascicle of the *Lotus Sutra*, in
which the bodhisattva proclaims his all-embracing compassion
and willingness to act on behalf of all suffering beings. He tells
the assembly that if anyone is in any need or trouble, whether
shipwreck, threat of bandits, storms, or other perils, all they
need do is call upon his name single-mindedly and he will deliver
them. In addition, he will grant the requests of all who pray to
him. In particular, he promises to grant a child to any woman
who prays to him for one, and the image of the 'child-granting
Kuan Yin' has become especially popular. Finally, he says that he
will assume any form in order to conform to the expectations and
inclinations of anyone in order to teach them the Dharma and
convert them; he might manifest as a Buddha, a high celestial
bodhisattva, a monk, a nun, a layman or laywoman, or even a
prostitute if required. In addition to these characteristics found
in the *Lotus Sutra*, the Pure Land traditions in China and Japan
revere Kuan Yin as one of the Three Holy Ones of Sukhavati. As
described in the *Meditation Sutra*, the *Larger Sukhdvati-vyuha
Sutra*, and the *Smaller Sukhavati-vyuha Sutra*, the Buddha
Amitabha presides over this Pure Land, and is assisted by the

two bodhisattvas Avalokitesvara and Mahasthamaprapta.
Kuan Yin's ability to appear in any form needed has led to a
profusion of iconographic representations. The bodhisattva can
be represented as both male and female as need and occasion
demand. The greatest number of variations appear within
esoteric scriptures, mandalas, and images, in which he can
appear in normal human shape, or with any number of heads,
eyes, and arms, and also in independent guises with different
names such as Chun-t'i. In one common practice, the devotee
recites the Great Compassion Mantra (Chinese, Ta pei chou) while
visualizing 108 separate forms of the bodhisattva in sequence.
The bodhisattva's broad compassion (karuna), all-embracing vows,
ability to manifest in various forms, and easy accessibility have
all served to make him the most widely called-upon source of
help not only in east Asian Buddhism, but in the folk beliefs of
all regions as well.

Kushan Empire

A dynasty established in north-west and central India by people
of Turkic origin who had earlier migrated from the Chinese
borders of central Asia. At its peak under Kanishka, the Kushan
territory extended from present-day Afghanistan as far east
as Magadha, but the empire was short-lived and disintegrated
by the end of the 3rd century CE. The Kushans were devout
adherents of Buddhism and were instrumental in supporting its
growth throughout India and its transmission to many parts of
central Asia.

Mahakashyapa

Also known as Kashyapa, an Arhat and senior disciple of the Buddha famed for his saintly and austere lifestyle and exceptional accomplishments. The Buddha regarded him as his equal in exhorting the monks, and in entering and abiding in the trances (dhyana). Mahakashyapa is said to have borne seven of the 32 marks of a superman (dvatrimsad-vara-laksana) on his body and was renowned for his supernatural powers (rddhi). He was not present at the Buddha's death and it is said that the funeral pyre refused to light until he arrived a week later. As the most senior monk present, he was nominated to act as president at the Council of Rajagrha that followed shortly after the Buddha's demise. At the council he personally questioned Ananda and Upali in order to establish which were the orthodox sutra and Vinaya teachings. He also brought certain charges against Ananda, including having interceded with the Buddha to allow the ordination of women, and of failing to request the Buddha to extend his life. Mahakashyapa is regarded by the Ch'an school as its first patriarch because he was the only one to grasp the meaning of a wordless sermon in which the Buddha simply held up a flower and smiled. The meaning of this gesture is that the truth is beyond all verbal explanation, and as such needs to be taught not through doctrines but by direct transmission from teacher to student.

Mahayana

Sanskrit for 'the great vehicle'. A major movement in the history of Buddhism embracing many schools in a sweeping reinterpretation of fundamental religious ideals, beliefs and values. Although there is no evidence for the existence of

Mahayana prior to the 2nd century CE, it can be assumed
that the movement began to crystallise earlier, incorporating
teachings of existing schools. Great emphasis is placed on the
twin values of compassion (karuna) and insight (prajna). The
bodhisattva who devotes himself to the service of others becomes
the new paradigm for religious practice, as opposed to the Arhat
who is criticized for leading a cloistered life devoted to the self-
interested pursuit of liberation. Schools which embraced the
earlier ideal are henceforth referred to disparagingly as the
Hinayana (Small Vehicle), or the Sravakayana (Vehicle of the
Hearers).

The philosophical teachings of the Mahayana are
adumbrated in a new body of literature known as the *Prajna-
paramita Sutras* or, *'Perfection of Insight'* texts. Here the
doctrine of emptiness (shunyata) comes to prominence, and the
Buddha is seen in a new light as a supernatural being who is
worthy of loving devotion. This new conception of his nature is
later formalized in the doctrine of the trikaya (three bodies). In
due course new teachings and schools arose under the umbrella
of the Mahayana such as the Madhyamaka, the Yogacara, the
Pure Land tradition, and the Vajrayana. The Mahayana form of
Buddhism is predominant in north Asia. It spread from India to
Nepal, Tibet, and central Asia, China, Korea, and Japan. Under
the influence of these cultures, it has taken many forms: the
Buddhism of Nepal and Tibet has been influenced by tantric
practices and the shamanism of central Asia, while in China
the influence of Taoism and Confucianism have left their mark.
The interaction between Buddhism and Taoism gave rise to the
Ch'an school of contemplative quietism which developed into
Japanese Zen.

Maitreya

One of the great mythical bodhisattvas whose cult was introduced into Buddhism at a fairly early date, and who is venerated in both Mahayana and non-Mahayana forms of Buddhism. Though his name signifies 'loving-kindness', some scholars suggest he was originally linked to the Iranian saviour-figure Mitra and that his later importance for Buddhists as the future Buddha currently residing in the Tusita heaven who will follow on from Sakyamuni Buddha derives from this source.

Manjushri

One of the great mythical or celestial bodhisattvas in Mahayana Buddhism, also known by the fuller name of Manjushri-kumara-bhuta. He is first mentioned in some of the early Mahayana texts such as the Prajna-paramita Sutras and through this connection soon came to symbolize the embodiment of insight (prajna). He later figures widely in many texts associated with tantric Buddhism such as the important Manjushri-mula-kalpa. Iconographically, he is depicted in a peaceful form holding a raised sword — symbolizing the power of insight — in his right hand and a book of the Prajna-paramita Sutra in his left. According to the tantras, he has a wrathful aspect, known as Yamantaka.

Maurya Empire

Early Indian dynasty centred on the state of Magadha which ruled from 324 to 184 BCE, although these dates and the chronology of the period as a whole are uncertain: the date of 184 is simply one of a number of guesses, and some authorities date the start of the dynasty to 313. The dynasty was founded

by Chandragupta who overthrew the preceding Nanda dynasty
and founded a capital at Pataliputra. He defeated the Greek king
Seleucus Nikator in 305 and as part of the terms of a marriage
treaty in 303 a Greek ambassador known as Megasthenes came
to reside at his court. Megasthenes composed a detailed account
of contemporary life in India which has not survived. According
to Buddhist accounts, Chandragupta converted to Jainism late in
life and went to south India where he starved himself to death
according to Jain custom. Chandragupta was succeeded by his
son Bindusara in 297. He extended the empire to include Mysore,
and by this time much of the subcontinent was under Mauryan
control with the exception of Kalinga (present-day Orissa).
Bindusara died in 272 and was succeeded by his son Ashoka,
who was consecrated in 268 (some modern authorities say 277)
and who conquered Kalinga and consolidated the greatest Indian
empire down to the time of the Moghuls and the British Raj. The
name Maurya derives from the word for a peacock.

Nirvana

The *summum bonum* of Buddhism and goal of the Eightfold Path.
The attainment of nirvana marks the end of cyclic existence
in samsara, the condition to which it forms the antithesis, and
in the context of which nirvana has to be understood. Samsara
is thus the problem to which nirvana is the solution. The word
nirvana is formed from the negative suffix nir and a Sanskrit
root which may be either 'va', meaning to blow, or 'vr', meaning
to cover. Both connote images of extinguishing a flame, in the
first case by blowing it out and in the second by smothering it
or starving it of fuel. Of these two etymologies, early sources
generally prefer the latter, suggesting that they understood

nirvana as a gradual process, like cutting off the fuel to a fire and letting the embers die down, rather than as a sudden or dramatic event. The popular notion that nirvana is the 'blowing out of a flame' is thus not widely supported in the canonical literature. In general, nirvana is described in negative terms as the end or absence of undesirable things, such as suffering (duhkha), although positive epithets also occur, notably the famous description of nirvana as the 'Unborn, Unoriginated, Uncreated, Unformed' found at *Udana* 8.3.

It is important to distinguish two kinds of nirvana: the first is the moral and spiritual transformation that takes place in life, and the second is the condition that subsists in the post-mortem state. The former is known as 'nirvana with remainder' (sopadisesa-nirvana) and the latter as 'nirvana without remainder' (anupadisesa-nirvana) or 'final nirvana' (parinirvana) although in the earliest sources nirvana and parinirvana are used interchangeably. The former is attained through the destruction of the defilements known as the outflows (asrava), and the latter is characterized by bringing to a halt for all time the dynamic activity of the psycho-physical factors (samskara) that compose the human individual. One in the latter condition is free from the effects of karma, but one in the former is not, although no new karma will be produced.

In Mahayana Buddhism, the bodhisattva ideal diminishes the importance of nirvana as a religious goal. This is because the bodhisattva makes a vow not to enter nirvana until all other beings have entered before him. Nirvana thus becomes a collective endeavour rather than a personal one. As new doctrinal positions emerge, moreover, the concept of nirvana undergoes development and is understood differently according to the philosophical perspective of the main schools. The Madhyamaka, for example, famously conclude that one who perceives emptiness (shunyata) as the true nature of phenomena will see nirvana and samsara as coterminous. The Yogacara school also teaches that the cessation of dualistic mental discrimination will lead to the realization that the opposition between nirvana and samsara is merely conceptual.

Schools such as Zen Buddhism also emphasize that for those who are awakened and perceive with insight (prajna), nirvana saturates every aspect of samsara. Certain texts also elaborate a distinction between two types of nirvana, mirroring the one made in the early sources between nirvana in this life and final nirvana. In the Mahayana these are known as localized (pratisthita) and unlocalized (apratisthita) nirvana. The latter corresponds to the state of pari-nirvana, but in the former a Buddha remains 'in the world but not of it', free of any attachment to samsara but accessible to help suffering beings.

Pali

The language of the texts of Theravada Buddhism. The Pali language is the product of the homogenization of the dialects in which the teachings of the Buddha were orally recorded and transmitted. The term Pali originally referred to a canonical text or passage rather than to a language. No script was ever developed for Pali and scribes used the scripts of their native languages to transcribe the texts. Tradition states that the language of the canon is Magadhi, the language believed to be spoken by Gautama Buddha.

Parinirvana

The 'final' or 'highest' nirvana, usually denoting the state of nirvana that is entered at death, in contrast to that attained during life. Also known as nirupadhi-sesa-nirvana. In the earliest sources nirvana and parinirvana are used interchangeably.

Pataliputra

Modern-day **Patna**, originally built by Ajatasatru and later the capital of the ancient Indian state of Magadha. Its key central location in north central India led rulers of successive dynasties to base their administrative capital here, from the Mauryans and the Guptas down to the Palas. In the Buddha's day it was a village known as Pataligama. He visited it shortly before his death and prophesied it would be great but would face destruction either by fire, water, or civil war. Two important councils were held here, the first at the death of the Buddha and the second in the reign of Ashoka. The city prospered under the Mauryas and a Greek ambassador Megasthenes resided there and left a detailed account of its splendour. The city also became a flourishing Buddhist center boasting a number of important monasteries. Known to the Greeks as Palibothra, it remained the capital throughout most of the Gupta dynasty (4th-6th centuries BCE). The city was largely in ruins when visited by Hsuan Tsang, and suffered further damage at the hands of Muslim raiders in the 12th century. Though parts of the city have been excavated, much of it still lies buried beneath modern Patna.

Prajna-paramita-ratna-guna-samcaya-gatha (The Accumulation of Precious Qualities)

(abbreviated as Rgs), 'Verses summarising the Precious Qualities of the Perfection of Wisdom', is a notable example of Buddhist Sanskrit literature at its earliest stage. It is probably the only extant text in Prajnaparamita literature written in the typical Buddhist Sanskrit language, it displays a number of unique grammatical forms and constructions, and is one of the earliest documents of Prajnaparamita thought.[6]

Samsara

The cycle of repeated birth and death that individuals undergo until they attain nirvana. The cycle, like the universe, is believed to have no beginning or end and individuals transmigrate from one existence to the next in accordance with their karma or moral conduct. Blinded by the three roots of evil (akusala-mula), namely greed, hatred, and delusion, beings are said to wander in samsara until such time as they are fortunate enough to hear the Dharma and put it into practice. The way this process of continuous rebirth occurs is explained step by step in the doctrine of Dependent Origination (pratitya-samutpada). Although not mentioned by name, samsara is the situation that is characterized as suffering (duhkha) in the first of the Four Noble Truths (aryasatya). The word samsara does not appear in the Vedas, but the notion of cyclic birth and death is an ancient one and dates to around 800 BCE. It is common to all mainstream Indian religions.

---

[6]   This definition is from: Akira Yuyama, ed., *Prajna-Paramita-Ratna-Guna-Samcaya-Gatha (Sanskrit Recension A)* (Cambridge: Cambridge University Press, 1976).

Sangha

The Buddhist community, especially those who have been ordained as monks (bhiksu) and nuns (bhiksuni) but originally referring to the 'fourfold sangha' of monks, nuns, laymen (upasaka), and laywomen (upasika). The minimal requirements for admission to the Sangha are faith in the 'three jewels' (triratna) of the Buddha, the Dharma, and the Sangha (in this context meaning the arya-sangha), usually demonstrated in the act of 'taking refuge'. Laymen are expected to keep the Five Precepts (panca-sila) while monks and nuns follow the Pratimoksa code of over 200 rules.

Sanskrit

The primary language of classical Indian literature, philosophy, and scripture. Its origins are uncertain since the earliest extant inscriptions are rather late. Though it has some links to the language of the Vedas, some scholars believe Sanskrit is an artificial language as the name suggests ('perfected', 'completed') compiled from various dialects and languages current in India during the 4th to 3rd centuries BCE. Commanding an enormous prestige and authority, it possesses a complex grammatical structure and a vast vocabulary suited to expressing subtle philosophical and religious concepts. Not used originally by Buddhists, it was adopted first by the Sarvastivada school and then later became the standard language for most Mahayana literature. A variant form, known to scholars as Buddhist Hybrid Sanskrit (BHS), was often used in Mahayana sutras. This is (like Pali) a form of Middle Indian with a relatively high level of Sanskritization.

Sariputra

The chief disciple of the Buddha. A lifelong friend of
Mahamaudgalyana, the two renounced the world on the
same day and first became disciples of the sceptic Sanjaya
Belatthiputta. Thereafter both converted to Buddhism, and on
the day of their ordination the Buddha declared them to be
his two chief disciples. Both soon became Arhats. The Buddha
declared Sariputra to be a perfect disciple and second only to
himself in transcendent knowledge (prajna). Sariputra frequently
preached with the Buddha's approval, and for his contribution
to the propagation of the faith was rewarded with the title
'General of the Dharma'. He had special expertise in analytical
philosophy and is regarded as the originator of the Abhi-dharma
tradition. Sariputra was renowned for his exemplary qualities
of compassion, (karuna), patience, and humility. He was older
than the Buddha and when he died a few months before him, the
Buddha pronounced a eulogy.

Shakyamuni

Literally 'the Sakyan sage'. A title of the Buddha, found
particularly in Mahayana sources where it distinguishes him
from the numerous other Buddhas mentioned in the sutras.

Shraddhotpada Mahayana Sutra (The Awakening of Faith in the Mahayana)

A short *summa* of Mahayana thought attributed to the Indian
Buddhist thinker and poet Ashvaghosha and translated
into Chinese in the year 550 CE by Paramartha. A second
translation, by Siksananda, was produced in the T'ang dynasty.
In spite of these two 'translations', no Indian original has

ever been discovered, and it is now certain that the text is an apocryphal work of Chinese origin. Despite its brevity and terseness, the work displays its author's brilliance at synthesizing many of the major ideas of Mahayana Buddhism, and so this treatise has exercised an enormous influence on east Asian Buddhist thought.

The text's major theme is the relationship between the noumenon (the absolute, enlightenment (bodhi), the universal, and the eternal) and phenomena (the relative, the unenlightened, the particular, and the temporal), and it poses the following questions. How are limited, ignorant beings to attain the bliss of wisdom? How shall the particular attain to the universal, the temporal to the eternal? To answer these questions, the treatise postulates a transcendent that pervades the immanent. The noumenon, called suchness (tathata) or absolute mind, does not exist in a pristine realm above and beyond phenomena, but expresses itself precisely as phenomena. The conjunction of the noumenal and the phenomenal occurs in the concept of the tathagata-garbha, or 'embryonic Buddha'. The term 'garbha', meaning both embryo and womb, denotes the simultaneous appearance of the goal sought (the embryo) and the conditions that make it possible (the womb). Suffering beings, in so far as they are suffering, remain deluded and in bondage. However, insofar as they are beings, they display their suchness and are aspects of the activity of absolute mind, and in this sense, they already contain the goal of transcendence and liberation within themselves.

These ideas are worked out in more detail through the use of the concepts of 'original enlightenment' and 'acquired enlightenment'. The first symbolizes the perfect and complete presence within all beings of ultimate reality and the absolute mind. The second serves as a recognition that, on the level of phenomena, suffering and ignorance (avidya) are real, and beings must still work to overcome them. However, because noumenon and phenomena do not exist separately, but only in and through each other, there is no unbridgeable gap between them; quite the contrary, they coincide completely. Because this is true, beings can gain enlightenment (bodhi) and liberation from suffering. The second half of the text presents practical suggestions for religious cultivation so that readers may develop faith (sraddha) and ultimately attain liberation. These exercises serve to correct flawed or biased views, and to increase the practitioner's faith and devotion.

Shunyata

Emptiness or nothingness, a concept mainly, but not exclusively, associated with the Mahayana. It has various particular nuances in the different Mahayana schools: according to the Madhyamaka, it is equivalent to Dependent Origination (pratitya-samutpada), while for the Yogacara it is the direct realization of the non-existence of a perceiving subject and perceived objects, said to be the natural state of the mind. In the philosophical doctrine of sunyavada ('the way of emptiness') it is not to be equated with nihilism since the term is equivalent in meaning to suchness (tathata) and ultimate reality or ultimate truth (dharma-dhatu). What is sometimes referred to as 'Great Emptiness' (maha-sunyata) is the abandonment of even the notion of emptiness.

Sravaka

Name given by the Mahayana to the early disciples who 'heard' the teachings of the Buddha and by practicing them sought to become Arhats. Like Hinayana, the term has a derogatory flavor (although in this case less pronounced) since the hearers are seen by the Mahayana as interested only in their personal salvation in contrast to the more altruistic path of the bodhisattvayana which aims at universal liberation. The term frequently occurs in the threefold classification of Sravakas, Pratyekabuddhas, and bodhisattvas, which represent the three main types of religious aspirant.

Subhuti

A minor figure in the early tradition, declared to be the chief among the disciples who dwell in remote places (aranaviharin). He becomes much more important in Mahayana Buddhism where he appears as chief interlocutor in many sutras, particularly in the early Perfection of Insight (Prajna-paramita) literature. There he is depicted as a wise bodhisattva who confounds the early disciples with his profound understanding of the doctrine of emptiness (sunyata).

Tathagata

A title or epithet of the Buddha. The term can mean either 'one who has thus come' or 'one who has thus gone'. The Buddha used the term to refer to himself after he had attained enlightenment (bodhi), and it became one of the stock epithets of a Buddha. Other honorific titles include Bhagavan (lord), Jina (conqueror), Arhat (worthy one), and Samyak-sambuddha (perfectly enlightened Buddha). The historical Buddha Siddhartha

Gautama was also known as Sakyamuni or 'the sage of the
Sakyas', and is commonly referred to this way in the Mahayana
tradition.

Tathata

Term meaning 'suchness', and denoting the way things are in
truth or actuality, and used especially in Mahayana Buddhism
to denote the essential nature of reality and the quiddity or
true mode of being of phenomena which is beyond the range
of conceptual thought (vikalpa). The term is one of a range of
synonyms for the absolute, which include emptiness (shunyata),
thusness (tattva), the limit of reality (bhuta-koti), and true
suchness (bhuta-tathata).

Techne

craft; practice; making or doing, as contrasted with episteme or
knowing.[7]

Theravada Buddhism

The only one of the early Buddhist schools of the Hinayana or
'Small Vehicle' to have survived down to modern times. Today,
the Theravada is the dominant tradition of Buddhism throughout
most of south-east Asia, particularly Sri Lanka, Burma,
Thailand, Laos, and Cambodia. According to tradition, the
school spread initially as the result of missionary activity after
being brought to Sri Lanka by Mahinda, the son of Ashoka. The
school claims its origins go back to the ancient body of the Elders
(sthaviras) before the separation from the Mahasamghikas, but
there is no historical evidence to support this. There are close

---

[7]   This definition is from Wiktionary, https://en.wiktionary.org/.

similarities, however, between the Theravada and the ancient Vibhajyavadins who were declared by Ashoka to be the orthodox party at the Council of Pataliputra II. The school is characterized by fidelity to the texts of the Pali Canon, the earliest complete set of Buddhist scriptures preserved intact in a single canonical language. Its attitude to doctrine and its outlook on social issues is generally conservative, although in modern times monks have come forward to challenge traditional attitudes.

Trichiliocosm

A concept in cosmology of a 'third-order' universe containing one thousand second-order clusters, which are made of one thousand first-order clusters, which are in turn made of a thousand worlds each. Billion-fold universe.[8]

Tushita

A heaven, home to the 'contented gods'. A day in this world is said to be equal to 400 years of human life. This particular heaven is distinguished by being the one in which bodhisattvas are reborn before they attain enlightenment (bodhi) in their next life as a human being. Graced by the presence of the bodhisattva, the Tusita heaven is the most beautiful of all the celestial worlds. It is now said to be the residence of the Buddha-to-be, Maitreya. In Mahayana cultures, those of more humble aspiration would seek rebirth not in Tusita but in the Pure Land of Amitabha.

---

[8]   Ibid.

Upanishad

An authorless Hindu religious and philosophical text considered to be an early source of the religion, found mostly as the concluding part of the Brahmanas and in the Aranyakas.[9]

Upaya kaushalya

The concept of 'skillful means' is of considerable importance in Mahayana Buddhism and is expounded at an early date in texts such as the *Upaya-kausalya Sutra*, the *Lotus Sutra*, and the *Teachings of Vimalaklrti Sutra* (*Vimalakirti-nirdesa Sutra*). In chapter two of the *Lotus Sutra* the Buddha introduces the doctrine of skillful means and demonstrates through the use of parables throughout the text why it is necessary for him to make use of stratagems and devices. The text depicts him as a wise man or kindly father whose words his foolish children refuse to heed. To encourage them to follow his advice he has recourse to 'skillful means', realizing that this is the only way to bring the ignorant and deluded into the path to liberation. Although this involves a certain degree of duplicity, such as telling lies, the Buddha is exonerated from all blame since his only motivation is compassionate concern for all beings.

At the root of the idea is the notion that the Buddha's teaching is essentially a provisional means to bring beings to enlightenment (bodhi) and that the teachings which he gives may vary: what may be appropriate at one time may not be so at another. The concept is used by the Mahayana to justify innovations in doctrine, and to portray the Buddha's early teachings as limited and restricted by the lesser spiritual potential of his early followers. In the Mahayana, skillful means

---

[9] Ibid.

comes to be a legitimate method to be employed by Buddhas and bodhisattvas whenever the benefit of beings warrants it. Spurred on by their great compassion (mahakaruna), bodhisattvas are seen in some sources (such as the *Upaya-kausalya Sutra*) breaking the precepts and committing actions that would otherwise attract moral censure. The assumption underlying the doctrine is that all teachings are in any case provisional and that once liberation is attained it will be seen that Buddhism as a body of philosophical doctrines and moral precepts was only of use as a means to reach the final goal and that its teachings do not have ultimate validity. The equivalent term in Pali sources (upaya-kosalla) is relatively rare and simply denotes the Buddha's skill in expounding the Dharma.

Vimalakirtinirdesa Sutra (The Teaching of Vimalakirti)

A Buddhist scripture that has been highly influential in east Asia. The Sanskrit title means *'The Teaching of Vimalakirti'*, and indeed the principal character and speaker throughout the work is not the Buddha or any high bodhisattva, but the layman Vimalakirti (Japanese, Yuima). The Sanskrit original was lost long ago, although fragments of it are preserved as quotations in other works, and recently the discovery of a Sanskrit manuscript in the Potala palace in Lhasa was announced in Japan. The work's many qualities — such as its eloquence, orderliness of exposition, and even humour — have made it a very popular text throughout the world of Mahayana Buddhism. According to its translator, Etienne Lamotte, the sutra 'is perhaps the crowning jewel of the Buddhist literature of the Great Vehicle'. He describes it as 'vibrating with life and full of humour', avoiding the prolixity of other Mahayana works while equalling them in the profundity of its teachings.

The sutra was translated into Chinese as early as 185 CE, (although this translation has been lost), and was translated six more times after that. The translation made by Kumarajiva around 406 (Taisho 475) is considered the standard among the three still extant. A Tibetan translation also exists, as do other translations (or retranslations from the Chinese or Tibetan) in other languages of central Asia. The primary topic of this sutra is the perfection of insight (Prajna-paramita) teachings of Mahayana Buddhism. It also concerns itself to refute Hinayana doctrine, as represented by the ten major disciples of the Buddha who are consistently reproved by Vimalakirti for their faulty understanding. One of the strengths of the sutra is that it teaches by action as well as by word. For example, while it teaches that the concepts of time and space are mere conventions, it also demonstrates this by several miraculous events: the great throng who call on Vimalakirti in his narrow room somehow all fit comfortably inside it; an entire Buddha-field (Buddha-ksetra) with all its inhabitants is shrunk so that it fits into the palm of the hand. The distinctions between monastic follower and lay follower and between Buddha and ordinary being are called into question by the person of Vimalakirti, a layman and ordinary man of the world who nevertheless rivals the bodhisattva Manjushri himself in understanding. The scripture also shows a mystical turn in its presentation of the Mahayana teaching of emptiness (shunyata). In one of the most famous scenes, called the 'thunderous silence of Vimalakirti', a debate ensued over the proper manner in which to teach this doctrine. After many participants — culminating with Manjushri — give their understanding, all turn to Vimalakirti to give the final word, at which point he keeps silent, eloquently demonstrating the ultimate failure of language to produce a proper understanding of reality. All of these features, along with the wry humour of many of the episodes (particularly those that produce the discomfiture of the Buddha's disciples) have made this sutra a favourite in east Asia, especially within the Ch'an and Zen schools.

Yuezhi

An ancient Indo-European people who originally settled in the arid grasslands of the eastern Tarim Basin area, in what is today Xinjiang and western Gansu, in China, before migrating to Transoxiana, Bactria and then northern South Asia, where one branch of the Yuezhi founded the Kushan Empire.

Yuima

Japanese name of the Indian sage Vimalakirti, a Buddhist layman who was renowned for his superior insight and wisdom.[10]

Zendo

A hall in a Zen monastery for the practice of zazen, or seated meditation.

---

[10] Definition derived from https://www.kimbellart.org/collection/ap-198202 (Kimbell Art Museum).

Figure 14. Kerolos Samy Yani, *Portrait of Roger Weir,* 2020, pencil sketch.

ABOUT THE AUTHOR

Roger Weir (1940-2018) was an American scholar and life-long educator. He was born and raised in Saginaw, Michigan. Due to health restrictions as a child, he spent much of his time reading — everything from Isaac Asimov to Edgar Rice Burroughs. This early reading would ultimately set the stage for a life of dedicated research and education. Weir received a Bachelor's of Science in philosophy from the University of Wisconsin — Madison in 1963. After graduating he took a couple of years off to independently study architecture and Chinese culture. In 1965 he enrolled in a master's program at San Francisco State College (now San Francisco State University). Weir earned a Master's of Arts in Interdisciplinary Studies in 1969. Shortly after graduating from SF State, Roger was recruited by Mount Royal College (now Mount Royal University) in Calgary, Canada to design and teach a special interdisciplinary curriculum. There he created a 16-part curriculum over the course of 5 years, and taught 9 courses himself. Weir returned to the U.S. in the mid-1970s, relocating to Los Angeles. Shortly thereafter he began delivering lectures at various local venues, including, the Philosophical Research Society, the Theosophical Society, and the Bodhi Tree Bookstore. Over the next four decades he delivered over two thousand recorded presentations, aided by his growing private library of over 80,000 volumes. Explore more content by Weir at, sharedpresencefoundation.org.

ABOUT SHARED PRESENCE FOUNDATION

The **Shared Presence Foundation,** founded in 2011, is driven to preserve and publicly disseminate Roger Weir's teachings and coursework. The Foundation has compiled, documented, and archived his voluminous work in order to make it available to current and future learners. The Foundation is also dedicated to publishing works of historical, artistic, and scientific insight. Experience thousands of lectures, transcripts, and more at: sharedpresencefoundation.org

DIRECTORY

ALEXANDRIA AND THE HELLENISTIC WORLDVIEW | 1984
PRESENTED AT WHIRLING RAINBOW, LOS ANGELES, CA
13 PRESENTATIONS

THE AMERICAN INDIANS AND THEIR SPIRIT WORLD | 1986
PRESENTED AT THE PHILOSOPHICAL RESEARCH SOCIETY,
LOS ANGELES, CA
SINGLE PRESENTATION

AN AMERICAN READING OF THE *BHAGAVAD GITA* | 1991
PRESENTED AT THE PHOENIX BOOKSTORE,
SANTA MONICA, CA
9 PRESENTATIONS

THE ANCIENT HERMETIC WRITINGS | 1990
PRESENTED AT THE PHILOSOPHICAL RESEARCH SOCIETY,
LOS ANGELES, CA
13 PRESENTATIONS

THE ANCIENT HERMETIC WRITINGS: BASED ON THE CORPUS HERMETICUM | 1990
PRESENTED AT THE PHOENIX BOOKSTORE,
SANTA MONICA, CA
SINGLE PRESENTATION

ARCHETYPAL STUDIES: A JUNGIAN COMMENTARY ON *THE BOOK OF DANIEL* | 1988
PRESENTED AT THE PHILOSOPHICAL RESEARCH SOCIETY, LOS ANGELES, CA
7 PRESENTATIONS

ARCHETYPAL STUDIES: AN ESOTERIC COMMENTARY ON *EPISTLE TO THE HEBREWS* | 1988
PRESENTED AT THE PHILOSOPHICAL RESEARCH SOCIETY, LOS ANGELES, CA
6 PRESENTATIONS

ARCHETYPAL STUDIES: C.G. JUNG AND W.B. YEATS | 1988
PRESENTED AT THE PHILOSOPHICAL RESEARCH SOCIETY, LOS ANGELES, CA
13 PRESENTATIONS

ARCHETYPAL STUDIES: HEINRICH ZIMMER AND JOSEPH CAMPBELL | 1988
PRESENTED AT THE PHILOSOPHICAL RESEARCH SOCIETY, LOS ANGELES, CA
13 PRESENTATIONS

THE ASCLEPIUS | 1984
PRESENTED AT THE GNOSTIC SOCIETY, LOS ANGELES, CA
SINGLE PRESENTATION

ASIAN SPIRITUAL CLASSICS, 300 CE TO THE PRESENT | 1982
PRESENTED AT THE PHILOSOPHICAL RESEARCH SOCIETY,
LOS ANGELES, CA
12 PRESENTATIONS

THE BODHISATTVA AND THE SPACE AGE: THE GREAT IDEA IN OUR TIME | 1982
PRESENTED AT THE PHILOSOPHICAL RESEARCH SOCIETY,
LOS ANGELES, CA
SINGLE PRESENTATION

BODHISATTVAS HERMETIC CHIVALRY | 2012
PRESENTED AT BODHI TREE BOOKSTORE,
WEST HOLLYWOOD, CA
12 PRESENTATIONS

BODHISATTVAS: THE DEVELOPMENT OF THE IDEA OF ENLIGHTENMENT-BEINGS, 250 BCE TO 750 CE | 1983
PRESENTED AT THE PHILOSOPHICAL RESEARCH SOCIETY,
LOS ANGELES, CA
13 PRESENTATIONS

C. G. JUNG'S ALCHEMICAL SOROR MYSTICA | 1987
PRESENTED AT THE GNOSTIC SOCIETY, LOS ANGELES, CA
SINGLE PRESENTATION

CH'AN TAOISM: THE CHINESE CONFIGURATION OF THE BUDDHA BY HUI NENG AND HUANG PO | 1987
PRESENTED AT THE PHILOSOPHICAL RESEARCH SOCIETY, LOS ANGELES, CA
SINGLE PRESENTATION

CHANG-AN: T'ANG DYNASTY CAPITAL AND MAGICAL TAOIST CITY | 1982
PRESENTED AT THE PHILOSOPHICAL RESEARCH SOCIETY, LOS ANGELES, CA
SINGLE PRESENTATION

CHRIST IN ALEXANDRIA | 1985
PRESENTED AT THE PHILOSOPHICAL RESEARCH SOCIETY, LOS ANGELES, CA
SINGLE PRESENTATION

THE CLASSIC GREEK SPIRIT | 1981
PRESENTED AT THE PHILOSOPHICAL RESEARCH SOCIETY, LOS ANGELES, CA
12 PRESENTATIONS

DANTE'S *PARADISE* AND THE MEANING OF PEACE | 1985
PRESENTED AT THE PHILOSOPHICAL RESEARCH SOCIETY, LOS ANGELES, CA
SINGLE PRESENTATION

THE DARK AGES MYTH: JUSTIN MARTYR TO ROGER BACON | 1984
PRESENTED AT WHIRLING RAINBOW, LOS ANGELES, CA
26 PRESENTATIONS

DEAD SEA SCROLLS | 1989
PRESENTED IN LOS ANGELES, CA
15 PRESENTATIONS

DIFFERENTIAL CONSCIOUSNESS | 1998–1999
PRESENTED AT BODHI TREE BOOKSTORE,
WEST HOLLYWOOD, CA
104 PRESENTATIONS

DIFFERENTIAL CONSCIOUSNESS | 2000–2001
PRESENTED AT BODHI TREE BOOKSTORE,
WEST HOLLYWOOD, CA
105 PRESENTATIONS

DIFFERENTIAL CYCLE | 1985
PRESENTED IN LOS ANGELES, CA
52 PRESENTATIONS

DIFFERENTIAL CYCLE | 1987
PRESENTED IN LOS ANGELES, CA
52 PRESENTATIONS

ECUMENE | 1988–1989
PRESENTED AT WHIRLING RAINBOW, LOS ANGELES, CA
53 PRESENTATIONS

ECUMENE | 1990–1991
PRESENTED AT WHIRLING RAINBOW, LOS ANGELES, CA
104 PRESENTATIONS

ECUMENE | 1996–1997
PRESENTED AT BODHI TREE BOOKSTORE,
WEST HOLLYWOOD, CA
104 PRESENTATIONS

ECUMENE; OR, PAIDEIA | 1994–1995
PRESENTED IN LOS ANGELES, CA
104 PRESENTATIONS

THE ENLIGHTENMENT | 1983
PRESENTED AT THE GNOSTIC SOCIETY, LOS ANGELES, CA
13 PRESENTATIONS

THE EUROPEAN EL DORADO, 1560 TO 1660: THE CENTURY OF A GOLDEN MYSTERY OF MAN | 1984
PRESENTED AT THE PHILOSOPHICAL RESEARCH SOCIETY,
LOS ANGELES, CA
13 PRESENTATIONS

EXPLORATION OF THE HERMETIC TRADITION | 1988
PRESENTED IN LOS ANGELES, CA
13 PRESENTATIONS

THE FUTURE AND THE NEW PAST | 2015
PRESENTED IN BEVERLY HILLS, CA
52 PRESENTATIONS

GANDHI | 1983
PRESENTED AT THE PHILOSOPHICAL RESEARCH SOCIETY,
LOS ANGELES, CA
13 PRESENTATIONS

GREAT SPIRITUAL CLASSICS OF THE ORIENT:
2500 BCE TO 300 CE | 1981
PRESENTED AT THE PHILOSOPHICAL RESEARCH SOCIETY,
LOS ANGELES, CA
13 PRESENTATIONS

HASTEEN KLAH: NAVAHO MEDICINE ARTIST | 1982
PRESENTED AT THE PHILOSOPHICAL RESEARCH SOCIETY,
LOS ANGELES, CA
SINGLE PRESENTATION

HERMES QUINTESSENTIAL | 2012
PRESENTED AT BODHI TREE BOOKSTORE,
WEST HOLLYWOOD, CA
4 PRESENTATIONS

HERMETIC AMERICA | 2008
PRESENTED AT BODHI TREE BOOKSTORE,
WEST HOLLYWOOD, CA
14 PRESENTATIONS

HERMETIC AMERICA — OUR CRITICAL HERITAGE:
JAMES FENIMORE COOPER, ABRAHAM LINCOLN,
HENRY ADAMS, MARK TWAIN | 1985
PRESENTED AT THE PHILOSOPHICAL RESEARCH SOCIETY,
LOS ANGELES, CA
13 PRESENTATIONS

HERMETIC AMERICA FUTURE | 2008
PRESENTED AT BODHI TREE BOOKSTORE,
WEST HOLLYWOOD, CA
13 PRESENTATIONS

HERMETIC AMERICA MATRIX: THE SYNTHESIZING VECTOR | 1987
PRESENTED AT THE PHILOSOPHICAL RESEARCH SOCIETY,
LOS ANGELES, CA
13 PRESENTATIONS

HERMETIC AMERICA STELLAR CIVILIZATION | 2013
PRESENTED IN BEVERLY HILLS, CA
52 PRESENTATIONS

HERMETIC AMERICA: A VISION OF OUR AMERICAN FUTURE | 1991
PRESENTED AT THE PHOENIX BOOKSTORE,
SANTA MONICA, CA
15 PRESENTATIONS

HERMETIC AMERICA: AMERICAN SPIRITUAL CLASSICS | 1982
PRESENTED AT THE PHILOSOPHICAL RESEARCH SOCIETY,
LOS ANGELES, CA
13 PRESENTATIONS

HERMETIC AMERICA: BENJAMIN FRANKLIN, THOMAS JEFFERSON, HENRY DAVID THOREAU | 1985
PRESENTED AT THE PHILOSOPHICAL RESEARCH SOCIETY, LOS ANGELES, CA
13 PRESENTATIONS

HERMETIC AMERICA: TRANSFORMATIONAL AMERICA | 1985
PRESENTED AT THE PHILOSOPHICAL RESEARCH SOCIETY, LOS ANGELES, CA
13 PRESENTATIONS

HERMETIC AMERICA: TWENTIETH CENTURY AMERICA | 1985
PRESENTED AT THE PHILOSOPHICAL RESEARCH SOCIETY, LOS ANGELES, CA
13 PRESENTATIONS

HERMETIC ANTIQUITY AND THE RISE OF THE MYSTERIOUS PERSON ARCHETYPE | 1987–1988
PRESENTED AT WHIRLING RAINBOW, LOS ANGELES, CA
26 PRESENTATIONS

HERMETIC BODHISATTVAS | 2012
PRESENTED AT BODHI TREE BOOKSTORE, WEST HOLLYWOOD, CA
16 PRESENTATIONS

HERMETIC BODHISATTVAS CHIVALRY | 2012
PRESENTED AT BODHI TREE BOOKSTORE,
WEST HOLLYWOOD, CA
16 PRESENTATIONS

HERMETIC JESUS | 1994
PRESENTED IN LOS ANGELES, CA
SINGLE PRESENTATION

HERMETIC TRADITION – NEW SERIES | 1986
PRESENTED AT THE PHILOSOPHICAL RESEARCH SOCIETY,
LOS ANGELES, CA
13 PRESENTATIONS

HERMETIC TRADITION: FROM OSIRIS TO BENJAMIN FRANKLIN, FROM EGYPT TO AMERICA | 1986
PRESENTED AT WHIRLING RAINBOW, LOS ANGELES, CA
24 PRESENTATIONS

HERMETIC TRADITION: FROM THE RENAISSANCE TO THE FOUNDING OF THE UNITED STATES | 1987
PRESENTED AT THE PHILOSOPHICAL RESEARCH SOCIETY,
LOS ANGELES, CA
13 PRESENTATIONS

HERMETICA | 1993
PRESENTED IN LOS ANGELES, CA
13 PRESENTATIONS

THE HERO: A MAGICAL THEME IN CONSCIOUSNESS | 1990
PRESENTED AT THE PHILOSOPHICAL RESEARCH SOCIETY,
LOS ANGELES, CA
13 PRESENTATIONS

THE HIGH DHARMA | 1987
PRESENTED AT THE PHILOSOPHICAL RESEARCH SOCIETY,
LOS ANGELES, CA
12 PRESENTATIONS

HOW A MANDALA WORKS: AN EXAMPLE OF SELF-UNFOLDMENT | 1989
PRESENTED AT THE PHILOSOPHICAL RESEARCH SOCIETY,
LOS ANGELES, CA
SINGLE PRESENTATION

THE I CHING | 1990
PRESENTED AT THE PHOENIX BOOKSTORE,
SANTA MONICA, CA
12 PRESENTATIONS

IMMORTALITY AS SEEN BY MODERN SCIENCE | 1983
PRESENTED AT THE PHILOSOPHICAL RESEARCH SOCIETY,
LOS ANGELES, CA
SINGLE PRESENTATION

INTEGRAL CYCLE | 1986
PRESENTED IN LOS ANGELES, CA
52 PRESENTATIONS

INTERCONNECTIONS OF THE SECRET SOCIETIES | 1983
PRESENTED AT THE ANNIE BESANT THEOSOPHICAL LODGE, HOLLYWOOD, CA AND THE PHILOSOPHICAL RESEARCH SOCIETY, LOS ANGELES, CA
2 PRESENTATIONS

INTERSTELLAR LEARNING | 2004–2005
PRESENTED AT BODHI TREE BOOKSTORE, WEST HOLLYWOOD, CA
105 PRESENTATIONS

AN INTRODUCTION TO THIRTEEN MAJOR WORKS OF THE UPANISHADS | 1989
PRESENTED AT THE PHILOSOPHICAL RESEARCH SOCIETY, LOS ANGELES, CA
13 PRESENTATIONS

ITALIAN RENAISSANCE | 1983
PRESENTED AT THE PHILOSOPHICAL RESEARCH SOCIETY, LOS ANGELES, CA
12 PRESENTATIONS

JESUS IN ALEXANDRIA | 1987
PRESENTED IN LOS ANGELES, CA
39 PRESENTATIONS

JESUS IN ALEXANDRIA | 1991
PRESENTED AT THE PHOENIX BOOKSTORE, SANTA MONICA, CA
13 PRESENTATIONS

JESUS IN ALEXANDRIA | 1992
PRESENTED AT THE PHOENIX BOOKSTORE,
SANTA MONICA, CA
13 PRESENTATIONS

JESUS IN ALEXANDRIA AND MARY MAGDALENE: THE ORIGINS OF SHARED PRESENCE | 2008
PRESENTED AT BODHI TREE BOOKSTORE,
WEST HOLLYWOOD, CA
13 PRESENTATIONS

JESUS IN ALEXANDRIA: FROM PYTHAGORAS THRU ISIS TO ST. JOHN'S *APOCALYPSE* | 1991
PRESENTED AT THE PHOENIX BOOKSTORE,
SANTA MONICA, CA
12 PRESENTATIONS

JESUS THE HIGH PRIEST OF THE MOST HIGH: ACCORDING TO APOLLOS OF ALEXANDRIA | 1987
PRESENTED AT THE PHILOSOPHICAL RESEARCH SOCIETY,
LOS ANGELES, CA
SINGLE PRESENTATION

THE KING AND QUEEN IN THE QUEST | 1981
PRESENTED AT THE PHILOSOPHICAL RESEARCH SOCIETY,
LOS ANGELES, CA
12 PRESENTATIONS

KING ARTHUR'S CHRISTMAS STORY: SIR GAWAIN AND THE GREEN KNIGHT, A MIDDLE ENGLISH CHRISTMAS SPIRITUAL CLASSIC | 1982
PRESENTED AT THE PHILOSOPHICAL RESEARCH SOCIETY,
LOS ANGELES, CA
SINGLE PRESENTATION

THE LEARNING CIVILIZATION | 2006–2007
PRESENTED AT BODHI TREE BOOKSTORE,
WEST HOLLYWOOD, CA
104 PRESENTATIONS

MAHAYANA CHRISTIANITY | 1986
PRESENTED AT THE PHILOSOPHICAL RESEARCH SOCIETY,
LOS ANGELES, CA
3 PRESENTATIONS

THE MAJJHIMA-NIKAYA (MIDDLE-LENGTH SAYINGS) OF THE BUDDHA | 1990
PRESENTED AT THE PHILOSOPHICAL RESEARCH SOCIETY,
LOS ANGELES, CA
13 PRESENTATIONS

MANLY P. HALL AND JOHN THE BAPTIST: FORERUNNERS OF MILLENIA | 1991
PRESENTED AT THE PHILOSOPHICAL RESEARCH SOCIETY,
LOS ANGELES, CA
SINGLE PRESENTATION

MANLY P. HALL'S *ORDERS OF THE QUEST* | 1981
PRESENTED AT THE PHILOSOPHICAL RESEARCH SOCIETY,
LOS ANGELES, CA
SINGLE PRESENTATION

MARY MAGDALENE AND JESUS' GREAT WAY | 2008
PRESENTED AT BODHI TREE BOOKSTORE,
WEST HOLLYWOOD, CA
13 PRESENTATIONS

MICHELANGELO (1475–1564) | 1983
PRESENTED AT THE PHILOSOPHICAL RESEARCH SOCIETY,
LOS ANGELES, CA
SINGLE PRESENTATION

THE MILLENNIAL ARCHETYPE | 1986
PRESENTED AT THE GNOSTIC SOCIETY, LOS ANGELES, CA
SINGLE PRESENTATION

MYSTERIUM CONIUNCTIONIS | 1986
PRESENTED AT THE GNOSTIC SOCIETY, LOS ANGELES, CA
SINGLE PRESENTATION

THE MYSTIC CENTURY | 1983
PRESENTED AT THE GNOSTIC SOCIETY, LOS ANGELES, CA
13 PRESENTATIONS

NEOPLATONISM: THE JOURNEY TO SELFLESSNESS | 1987
PRESENTED IN LOS ANGELES, CA
SINGLE PRESENTATION

A NEW AION: FOUR TALKS ON OUR ONCE AND FUTURE WHOLENESS | 1994
PRESENTED AT BODHI TREE BOOKSTORE,
WEST HOLLYWOOD, CA
4 PRESENTATIONS

NEW TESTAMENT WISDOM FOR TODAY'S WORLD | 1982
PRESENTED IN LOS ANGELES, CA
7 PRESENTATIONS

ORIGINS OF HERMETIC SCIENCE | 1983
PRESENTED AT THE GNOSTIC SOCIETY, LOS ANGELES, CA
14 PRESENTATIONS

OUR OLD AION | 2012
PRESENTED AT BODHI TREE BOOKSTORE,
WEST HOLLYWOOD, CA
4 PRESENTATIONS

THE PARAYANA | 2009
PRESENTED AT BODHI TREE BOOKSTORE,
WEST HOLLYWOOD, CA
13 PRESENTATIONS

PARAYANA: REFRESHING THE WAY INTO THE HIGH DHARMA | 2014
PRESENTED IN BEVERLY HILLS, CA
52 PRESENTATIONS

PLATO | 1990
PRESENTED AT THE PHILOSOPHICAL RESEARCH SOCIETY,
LOS ANGELES, CA
13 PRESENTATIONS

PLATO II | 1991
PRESENTED AT THE PHILOSOPHICAL RESEARCH SOCIETY,
LOS ANGELES, CA
13 PRESENTATIONS

PLATO'S *THEORY OF EDUCATION* | 1990
PRESENTED AT THE PHILOSOPHICAL RESEARCH SOCIETY,
LOS ANGELES, CA
SINGLE PRESENTATION

PLOTINUS AND PATANJALI: PATTERNING TOWARD REALIZATION | 1984
PRESENTED AT THE PHILOSOPHICAL RESEARCH SOCIETY,
LOS ANGELES, CA
SINGLE PRESENTATION

PLOTINUS: THE HIGH WISDOM OF THE CLASSIC WEST | 1989
PRESENTED AT THE PHILOSOPHICAL RESEARCH SOCIETY,
LOS ANGELES, CA
13 PRESENTATIONS

PRELUDE TO THE TWENTIETH CENTURY | 1984
PRESENTED AT THE PHILOSOPHICAL RESEARCH SOCIETY,
LOS ANGELES, CA
13 PRESENTATIONS

PRIMORDIAL IMAGE BASE | 1981
PRESENTED AT THE PHILOSOPHICAL RESEARCH SOCIETY,
LOS ANGELES, CA
13 PRESENTATIONS

PTOLEMAIC ALEXANDRIA | 1980
PRESENTED IN LOS ANGELES, CA
SINGLE PRESENTATION

PTOLEMAIC ALEXANDRIA | 1982
PRESENTED AT THE PHILOSOPHICAL RESEARCH SOCIETY,
LOS ANGELES, CA
SINGLE PRESENTATION

THE PYRAMID TEXTS IN EGYPTIAN RELIGION | 1988
PRESENTED AT THE PHILOSOPHICAL RESEARCH SOCIETY,
LOS ANGELES, CA
13 PRESENTATIONS

PYTHAGORAS: WESTERN TRADITIONS OF THE SAGE | 1989
PRESENTED AT THE PHILOSOPHICAL RESEARCH SOCIETY,
LOS ANGELES, CA
13 PRESENTATIONS

QUINTESSENTIAL DIMENSIONS OF CONSCIOUSNESS | 2009
PRESENTED AT BODHI TREE BOOKSTORE,
WEST HOLLYWOOD, CA
13 PRESENTATIONS

SHARED PRESENCE | 1991
PRESENTED IN LOS ANGELES, CA
13 PRESENTATIONS

SHARED PRESENCE | 2009
PRESENTED AT BODHI TREE BOOKSTORE,
WEST HOLLYWOOD, CA
13 PRESENTATIONS

SHARED PRESENCE PEOPLE | 1994
PRESENTED IN LOS ANGELES, CA
4 PRESENTATIONS

SHARED-PRESENCE BODHISATTVAS | 1991
PRESENTED AT BRUCHION CENTER FOR ART, AND GNOSIS,
LOS ANGELES, CA
13 PRESENTATIONS

SPECIAL THANKSGIVING LECTURE:
C. G. JUNG | 1984
PRESENTED IN LOS ANGELES, CA
SINGLE PRESENTATION

SPIRITUAL CLASSICS OF THE EARLY
MIDDLE AGES: FROM PLOTINUS TO THE
BOOK OF KELLS | 1982
PRESENTED AT THE PHILOSOPHICAL RESEARCH SOCIETY,
LOS ANGELES, CA
10 PRESENTATIONS

SPIRITUAL CLASSICS OF THE LATE MIDDLE AGES | 1983
PRESENTED AT THE PHILOSOPHICAL RESEARCH SOCIETY, LOS ANGELES, CA
13 PRESENTATIONS

SPIRITUAL PERSONALITY: DEVELOPMENT AND PATTERN WITHIN HUMAN INTELLIGENCE | 1992–1993
PRESENTED AT WHIRLING RAINBOW, LOS ANGELES, CA
104 PRESENTATIONS

STAR WISDOM HUMANITY — PAIRED PHASE TRANSFORMS | 2010
PRESENTED AT BODHI TREE BOOKSTORE, WEST HOLLYWOOD, CA
52 PRESENTATIONS

STAR WISDOM MAN | 2009
PRESENTED AT BODHI TREE BOOKSTORE, WEST HOLLYWOOD, CA
13 PRESENTATIONS

STELLAR CIVILIZATION | 2002–2003
PRESENTED AT BODHI TREE BOOKSTORE, WEST HOLLYWOOD, CA
104 PRESENTATIONS

SUMMER SOLSTICE | 1981
PRESENTED AT THE PHILOSOPHICAL RESEARCH SOCIETY, LOS ANGELES, CA
SINGLE PRESENTATION

SUMMER SOLSTICE | 1982
PRESENTED IN LOS ANGELES, CA
SINGLE PRESENTATION

SUMMER SOLSTICE | 1983
PRESENTED IN LOS ANGELES, CA
SINGLE PRESENTATION

SUMMER SOLSTICE | 1984
PRESENTED IN LOS ANGELES, CA
SINGLE PRESENTATION

SUMMER SOLSTICE | 1988
PRESENTED IN LOS ANGELES, CA
SINGLE PRESENTATION

SUMMER SOLSTICE CELEBRATION | 1982
PRESENTED AT THE PHILOSOPHICAL RESEARCH SOCIETY,
LOS ANGELES, CA
SINGLE PRESENTATION

SUMMER SOLSTICE: THEODORE STURGEON MEMORIAL | 1985
PRESENTED IN LOS ANGELES, CA
SINGLE PRESENTATION

SUNDAY SERMON: AMERICAN VISION FUTURE | 1991
PRESENTED AT THE PHILOSOPHICAL RESEARCH SOCIETY,
LOS ANGELES, CA
SINGLE PRESENTATION

SYMBOLISM | 1980
PRESENTED AT THE PHILOSOPHICAL RESEARCH SOCIETY,
LOS ANGELES, CA
12 PRESENTATIONS

THE TAO OF JOURNEYING | 1980
PRESENTED AT THE PHILOSOPHICAL RESEARCH SOCIETY,
LOS ANGELES, CA
SINGLE PRESENTATION

TAO TE CHING | 1992
PRESENTED AT THE PHOENIX BOOKSTORE,
SANTA MONICA, CA
24 PRESENTATIONS

TAOISM | 1986
PRESENTED IN LOS ANGELES, CA
13 PRESENTATIONS

THE TAOIST TRADITION | 1986
PRESENTED AT THE PHILOSOPHICAL RESEARCH SOCIETY,
LOS ANGELES, CA
13 PRESENTATIONS

THE TAOIST TRADITION (CONTINUED) | 1986
PRESENTED AT THE PHILOSOPHICAL RESEARCH SOCIETY,
LOS ANGELES, CA
13 PRESENTATIONS

THOMAS BANYACYA – HOPI CHIEF | 1985
PRESENTED IN LOS ANGELES, CA
SINGLE PRESENTATION

THE TWENTIETH CENTURY | 1984

PRESENTED AT THE PHILOSOPHICAL RESEARCH SOCIETY,
LOS ANGELES, CA

13 PRESENTATIONS

INDEX